THE CACTI

OF

CALIFORNIA

BY

E. YALE DAWSON

WITH PHOTOGRAPHS BY DON SKINNER

UNIVERSITY OF CALIFORNIA PRESS
BERKELEY, LOS ANGELES, LONDON

CALIFORNIA NATURAL HISTORY GUIDES

Arthur C. Smith, General Editor

UNIVERSITY OF CALIFORNIA PRESS
BERKELEY AND LOS ANGELES, CALIFORNIA
UNIVERSITY OF CALIFORNIA PRESS, LTD.
LONDON, ENGLAND

CONTENTS

NOTE ON ILLUSTRATIONS — The cover portrays the Beaver Tail Cactus (*Opuntia basilaris*) in the foreground and the Pancake Pear (*Opuntia chlorotica*) in the background. Most of the color photographs are the work of Don Skinner, who also generously provided textual information through his long experience with California cacti. David L. Walkington, of California State College at Fullerton, provided information and photographs for the interior members of the prickly pear group, and Dr. Ralph Philbrick, of the Santa Barbara Botanic Garden, for the coastal species. Several color photographs are from the Homer Rush collection. Photographs of *Opuntia bigelovii* and *Ferocactus acanthodes* were taken by Dallas Clites. Some of the line drawings were reproduced from the early works of George Engelmann, some from *The Cactaceae* by Britton and Rose, and some from the writer's *How to Know the Cacti*, by permission of the Wm. C. Brown Co.

INTRODUCTION

The study of cacti in California has had a long history. Except for the prickly pear of the Atlantic states, known to Linnaeus, and four species from the upper Missouri River described in 1814 as a result of the exploration of the Louisiana Purchase, the first cacti in this country to be known to science came from San Diego. In 1834 Thomas Nuttall, pioneer of western American botany, discovered in the village of San Diego, then little more than the Mexican mission and its Indians, *"Echinocactus viridescens"* and *"Cereus californicus."*

By 1856, through the work of George Engelmann of St. Louis on collections obtained by the Pacific Railroad Survey and the explorations of the Mexican Boundary Commission, knowledge of California cacti was spreading rapidly. By 1919, when the first volume of the monumental monograph on Cactaceae by Britton and Rose was being published, a large body of information on California cacti had accumulated, and our deserts had been extensively explored.

A number of kinds had eluded the botanists, however, and these have continued to be discovered and described down to the present day. A new publication lies before me, just received in the mail, in which a new species of California prickly pear is named. Its characters have been confused or overlooked all these years and only now are clearly recognized. Similarly, the careful exploration of our desert ranges along the Arizona and Mexican boundaries has revealed very recently the occurrence in California of species hitherto known only from these other areas. Two of these are reported for the first time in this handbook. Perhaps you may find still others.

[5]

The more we explore and the more we learn of the cacti, the less certain we become of just how many kinds there are. Most of the species that were discovered many years ago appeared to be distinct from one another, but as collections expanded and observations became more critical, we noted numerous intergradations and intermediate conditions. Thus, where three species had been named earlier, we may now recognize only one, perhaps in three major variable groups that merge. Furthermore, we are increasingly aware that evolution in the cacti is going on before our eyes, that distinct species (and even genera) in nature are occasionally producing crosses that survive and become, in fact, new species. We have sometimes hastened this process by artificial introduction of species from other areas, particularly the Mission Cactus. The resulting hybridization with native species has added many variables to original natural populations.

Some of the difficulties in recognizing species among these variable cacti are related to their widespread distribution and variation in far-flung geographic areas. As a "broad" species may have a varied population in Texas, another in Arizona, and still another in California, so the California plants may scarcely resemble the Texas plants, yet may be linked by intermediates. Interpretations by different botanists of these variations have led to the use of different scientific names in designating the plants; so do not be dismayed if the name used here does not take the form that appears in another book. We have chosen names that, for a local flora, seem most convenient and useful in designating the California plants. A flora of North America would take a different point of view.

WHAT ARE CACTI?

The cacti of California provide an interesting and comprehensive assortment of members of a unique plant family. There are representatives in the driest, hot deserts; others live in foggy coastal scrub, beside high glacial lakes in the sierra, or in moist coniferous forests. But these are not all the habitats occupied by these remarkable plants.

The cacti are exclusively American plants. Although we find them scattered over much of the world today, those outside America have been carried about and planted since the first European saw a cactus when he disembarked with Columbus at Hispaniola. The first cacti brought to Europe were tropical kinds, and, indeed, the Cactaceae are most widespread in the American tropics, both in the dry and the wet. They grow not only in the tropical deserts of Peru, but in some very wet forests, often epiphytic on trees with orchids and bromeliads. They range all the way from Ecuador south into Patagonia and north into central Canada. They are on most of the Caribbean islands; and in the Galápagos Islands they got as far from the continent as 600 miles, but no farther.

The form of the cacti varies as much as the habitat. Some are spiny, woody, deciduous trees which look no more like the usual succulent cactus than does a rosebush, and there are vinelike, climbing forms that may festoon a forest. In short, we cannot always tell a cactus by its shape. All the cacti, however, have a peculiar structure called the areole.

The areoles are the little spots on the stems of cacti from which the spines arise. These specialized growth centers also produce the flowers and new branches. They usually bear one or more distinct spines, but may instead bear wool, hairs, bristles, or microscopic spines called glochids. In the prickly pears and chollas the true nature of the areole may be seen in young growth, for beside each areole of a young branch is a small, fleshy, awl-shaped structure which is really the leaf (fig. 1). The areole is in its axil and

[7]

represents a bud. This little leaf soon falls off, and in many cacti the leaves are not evident except microscopically, but the areole remains as the place at which growth and reproduction take place.

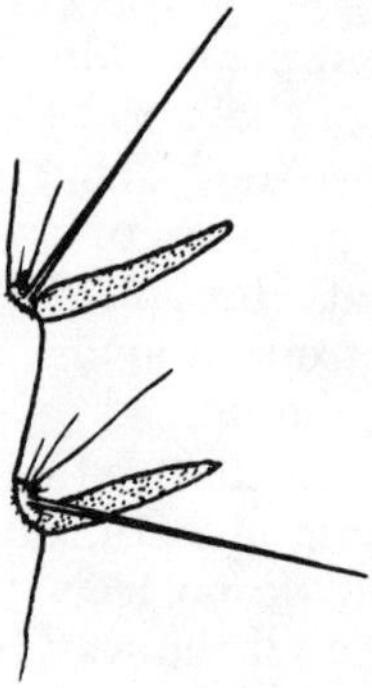

Fig. 1. Young areoles of *Opuntia*, showing spines in axils of awl-shaped leaves.

The flowers of cacti vary greatly in size, color, and form, but they have several characters in common. Except sometimes in our own *Mammillaria dioica*, the flowers are all perfect, having male and female parts. The ovary is inferior; there are numerous stamens; there is a single style with several stigma lobes; the petals and sepals, of indefinite number and little distinction, are called perianth segments (fig. 2). If a succulent plant has these various floral characters as well as the areoles, it is a cactus. Many succulents that are commonly mistaken for cacti (century plants, yuccas, ocotillo, euphorbias, etc.) can easily be distinguished by these features.

Spines provide many of the characters by which cactus species and genera are distinguished. Some areoles contain a single type of spine and others contain several. The areole usually has some kind of sharp, stiff spine, whether straight, curved, hooked, smooth, ribbed, cylindrical, or flattened. The spines are commonly arranged in a central position and (or)

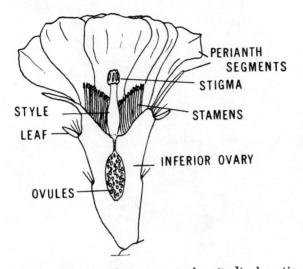

Fig. 2. A flower of *Opuntia* in longitudinal section, showing various parts.

in a radial position (fig. 3). Most genera have spines that are sharply pointed but not barbed. In most of the chollas, however, the spine is minutely barbed and provided with a sheath. In addition to the larger, stiffer spines, there are finer spines. The glochid, which is prevalent in *Opuntia* (fig. 4), is a minutely barbed, almost microscopic spine usually present in large numbers somewhat in the form of a packet. Some areoles contain mainly curly wool, hair, or fine felt forming a kind of pad, sometimes in addition to the heavy spines.

The position of the spines is often important, whether superficial, or on ribs, or crowning low tubercles or nipple-like, elongated tubercules (fig. 5). We have examples of all these types.

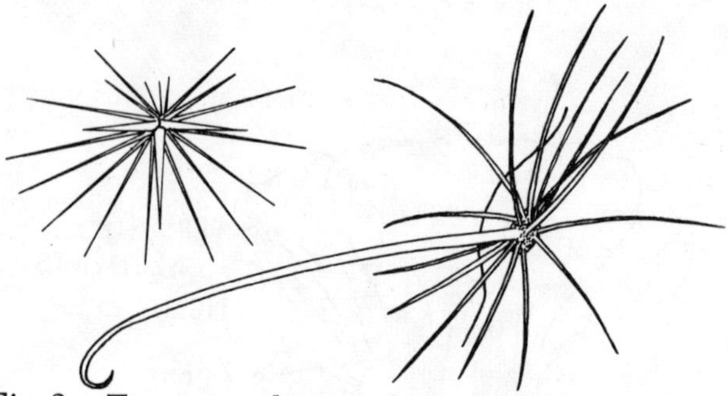

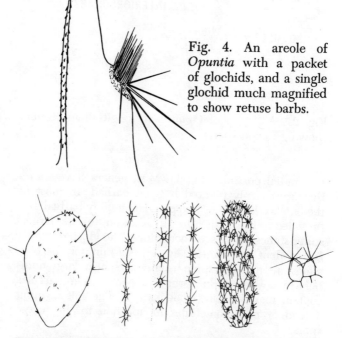

Fig. 3.　Two spine clusters, showing central and radial spines.

Fig. 4. An areole of *Opuntia* with a packet of glochids, and a single glochid much magnified to show retuse barbs.

Fig. 5. Various positions of spines, left to right: superficial, as in the prickly pears; on ribs, as in the saguaro; on tubercles, as in *Opuntia prolifera;* on nipples, as in *Mammillaria.*

The fruits are of diverse character in various genera. Some are both fleshy and spiny at maturity; others turn dry and shed seeds without going through a stage of soft pulp. Some lose their spines upon ripening and yield a fruit as sweet and innocuous as a strawberry. Others never bear spines and resemble an elongate berry (figs. 6, 25).

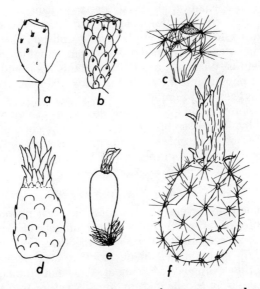

Fig. 6. Various kinds of cactus fruits: a, smooth and fleshy, with glochids (*Opuntia*); b, fleshy, tuberculate, with glochids (*Opuntia*); c. dry tuberculate (*Opuntia*); d. dry scaly (*Ferocactus*); e. fleshy, smooth, spineless (*Mammillaria*); f, fleshy and spiny (*Echinocereus*).

How to Study California Cacti

California wild flowers, including the cacti, are protected by law. In national and state parks, national forests, and in state and some county rights of way, collection of cacti is strictly forbidden. In some counties cacti cannot be collected even on private property without the written permission of the owner. These protective measures have become necessary to insure the perpetuation of these curious plants, many of which were fast disappearing into gardens, and later into trash cans. Living plants may still be collected in some areas by special permit, but usually only for scientific purposes. Most users of this book will study and photograph the cacti, but leave them for the next desert visitor to enjoy.

Photography of cacti in flower is an interesting hobby. The assembly of a complete collection of color slides of California cacti in flower is a challenge to any nature photographer, and his travels to this end are bound to yield exciting experiences.

Where to Find Them

There are several easily accessible areas in southern California in which fairly large numbers of different kinds of cacti may be observed together. For the several species confined to our south coastal region the Cabrillo National Monument on Point Loma, San Diego, is an excellent study area. A nature trail marks various kinds of cacti, and others may be seen within a few hundred yards of the lighthouse.

Most of the interior species of the southernmost desert parts of California may be seen along Highway 78 from Banner down Sentenac Canyon. Another cactus-rich route is Highway 80 from just east of Jacumba to the desert floor near Ocotillo. The lower reaches of the Pines-to-Palms Highway 74 also have cactus species of the Colorado Desert region in abundance.

[12]

The cactus flora of the more elevated Mojave Desert is distinct and may best be seen in the Joshua Tree National Monument, which has been set aside for the preservation of the desert flora. From near Whitewater on Highway 10 to Morongo one passes most of the Colorado Desert forms again, but beyond the Little San Bernardino Mountains the cacti of the high Mojave are found. The National Monument has an outstanding natural cactus exhibit area known as Cholla Cactus Garden.

The cactus flora of the far northeastern Mojave Desert, which includes several species not otherwise known within the state, is best seen along or just off Highway 15, the Las Vegas route, near Clark Mountain and the Ivanpah Mountains. Short side trips into such areas as Landfair Valley near Ivanpah may reveal unusual plants.

Several cacti occur in isolated localities in outlying areas. The notes under each plant name in the text will help you to find these localized kinds.

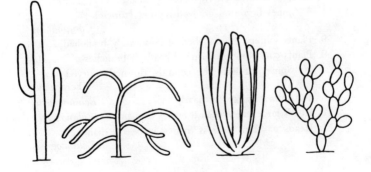

1. Plants gigantic, columnar, 8 to 30 feet tall .. *Carnegiea*
1. Plants smaller, not columnar, usually less than 6 feet tall. 2
   2. Plants with flat branches
                           Opuntia, subgenus *Platyopuntia*
   2. Plants globular, or cylindrical,
                 or with cylindrical branches 3
3. Plants cylindrical, the branches or main axis many times as long as broad 4
3. Plants globular or short-cylindrical; if branched, the branches only once or a few times as long as broad .. 5
   4. Areoles with glochids; spines usually barbed and with sheaths .... *Opuntia*, subgenus *Cylindropuntia*
   4. Areoles without glochids; spines neither barbed nor with sheaths .... *Bergerocactus*
5. Plants with hooked spines 6
5. Plants with spines straight or curved but not hooked .. 8
   6. Plants 4 inches or more in diameter; hooked spines several inches long .... *Sclerocactus*
   6. Plants, or their branches, less than 3 inches in diameter; hooked spines less than 2 inches long 7
7. Radial spines more than 30; seeds with a corky base
                           Phellosperma
7. Radial spines less than 30; seeds without a corky base
                           Mammillaria
   8. Spines borne on ribs ..../............. 9
   8. Spines borne on grooved nipples (tubercles)
                           Coryphantha
9. Plants solitary, unbranched or only rarely branched .. 10
9. Plants consisting of clustered heads or branches 11
   10. Spines, at least the centrals, distinctly curved
                           Ferocactus
   10. Spines straight or nearly so .... *Echinomastus*
11. Heads large, more than 6 inches in diameter. *Echinocactus*
11. Heads or branches less than 4 inches in diameter
                           Echinocereus

THE CACTI OF CALIFORNIA

OPUNTIA

Opuntia, our largest cactus genus, includes well over half of the species in the state. The opuntias are distributed almost everywhere cacti grow, from Canada to Patagonia. This large assemblage has two features by which all may be recognized: small awl-shaped leaves are present on young growth; and glochids are borne in the areoles. The several hundred species are divided into two easily recognized subgenera: *Cylindropuntia*, with cylindrical stems; and *Platyopuntia*, in which the stems or joints are flattened pads that are often mistakenly called leaves.

CYLINDROPUNTIA: THE CHOLLAS

Cholla is a Mexican name for the viciously spiny, cylindrical opuntias in which the spines are usually covered by a papery sheath, but are insidiously barbed. The vegetable kingdom has not produced anything else so fearfully armed. But in the desert one thing is worse than any pain of spine in the flesh. It is thirst. I have seen emaciated, dreadfully dehydrated cattle, deprived of water for months in the blistering heat, so mad from thirst that they eat the terrible cholla. They munch these awful morsels of moisture until their lips are pinned together with the spines, and their throats are a veritable pincushion. The spines eventually cause their death.

Pencil Cactus (*Opuntia ramosissima*)

The name "ramosissima," which means "exceedingly much branched," aptly describes this bushy plant. It forms a loose or dense shrub, usually 2 to 3 feet high,

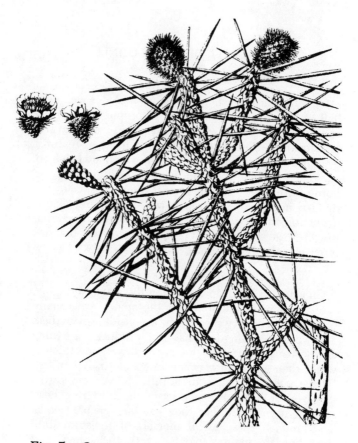

Fig. 7. *Opuntia ramosissima*, showing long, sheathed spines and pencil-like branches, and the spiny flowers and fruits.

consisting of a multitude of small cylindrical branches, about one-fourth of an inch in diameter, covered with diamond-shaped plates from which project, here and there, solitary spines 1½ to 2 inches long (fig. 7). A papery sheath, like the scabbard of a sword, encloses each spine, and this may easily be pulled off. Although most plants are densely spiny, some forms occur with few or no spines. The plant is not very succulent; after the first season's growth, the branches become woody.

The flowers are exceedingly variable in color, from greenish through yellow, reddish, and brown (pl. 1, a). They commonly appear during the midsummer desert heat of June and July, although flowering plants have been observed as early as April. The dry, spiny fruits have been likened to sand burrs.

Opuntia ramosissima is a plant of the desert floor and of alluvial washes generally below 3,000 feet. It is abundant throughout the southern Mojave Desert, the Colorado Desert, and the Borrego Valley. Some of the finest stands are east of Desert Center on Highway 10. In that area the plants become very large and bushy, even arborescent, and up to 6 feet tall. Some places support almost pure growths of this species as a unique desert shrubland.

In the area west of Lucerne Valley occurs the variety *denudata*, in which the long central spines are sparse or nearly absent.

Jumping Cholla; Teddy Bear Cactus
(*Opuntia bigelovii*)

Many an unwary easterner has seen this glistening plant as he enters California through the southeastern deserts, and has stopped to get a piece of what seems, from a distance, to be covered with soft, silvery bristles like a teddy bear. To his surprise the cactus jumps at him, or so he believes, and impales him on sharp spines. The spines are doubly wicked, for, being barbed, at the slightest touch they penetrate the flesh and are extracted with difficulty and pain. Pliers are usually required. The barbed spines, if broken off in the flesh, may, unless they fester out, travel through the body for months and emerge far from the place of entry. The joints, also, detach readily and litter the ground where the species grows; so one must be cautious not to brush against them with shoe or pant cuff.

Opuntia bigelovii is usually recognized easily by its treelike form and thick, densely spiny branches (pl. 1, *b*). The plant may reach a height of 6 to 8 feet, but is usually 3 to 4 feet tall, with silvery upper parts and dark, dingy trunk and old branch bases. The yellowish flowers with lavender streaks (pl. 1, *c*) appear during April, but are not conspicuous.

The Jumping Cholla is widely distributed through the southern Mojave Desert and Colorado Desert, where it grows on the lower slopes and alluvial fans of the desert hills usually below 3,000 feet. Good stands can be seen around Whitewater, near Palm Springs, and throughout much of the Anza-Borrego Desert State Park. An outstanding colony of this species occurs in the Joshua Tree National Monument's Cholla Cactus Garden.

Opuntia bigelovii has apparently produced at least two natural hybrids with other California chollas. In Mason Valley and Vallecito in San Diego County, a colony known as *O.* × *fosbergii* seems to be a hybrid with *O. echinocarpa* and to exhibit intermediate characters. A somewhat similar supposed hybrid with *O. acanthocarpa*, called *O.* × *munzii*, is known from Beal's Well Wash in the Chocolate Mountains of Imperial County.

Coast Cholla (*Opuntia prolifera*)

Along coastal hills and bluffs from Ventura to Baja California and on the Channel Islands one frequently

[18]

sees a small treelike cholla with abundant, persistent green fruits. This is *Opuntia prolifera,* so named for the fruits, which are proliferous and grow one upon another in series. It is easily recognized. Since its range is restricted to the coast and the islands, it never extends far enough inland to be confused with the desert species. In San Diego County, where it sometimes mingles with another coastal species, *O. serpentina,* it is distinguished by its erect, treelike habit. Plants may reach a height of 6 feet, but are usually 2 to 3 feet tall.

The flowers are rose red to purplish (pl. 2, *a*), appearing in spring, but too small to be conspicuous. The fruits are almost always sterile and usually bear more flowers at the next season, as if they were branches. This may continue for several years until the mass of persistent fruits, forming short, pendant chains, becomes so heavy as to break the bearing branch. As in *O. bigelovii,* the joints (fig. 5) are readily detached and often litter the ground, where many take root to produce new plants.

This species may be observed on the few remaining undeveloped chaparral hillslopes along Highway 101 in Orange and San Diego counties, such as those north of Laguna Beach and Newport Beach. It occurs on the nature trail in the Cabrillo National Monument.

Silver Cholla; Golden Cholla
(*Opuntia echinocarpa*)

This is the widest ranging, commonest, and most variable of the California chollas, extending from Mono County to Mexico and eastward into Utah and Arizona. In areas of its best development it is characterized by an erect habit, growing 3 to 4 feet tall, with a distinct trunk and a dense crown of cylindrical branches whose joints are mostly 4 to 6 inches long and in part readily detached. The young branches are exceedingly spiny; the spines usually have silvery or

[19]

yellow sheaths that give sparkle and color to the plant (pl. 1, *f*). Unlike its near relative, *Opuntia acanthocarpa*, this species has short tubercles only once or twice as long as broad, and a denser spination.

The flowers, although variable, are generally greenish-yellow with a reddish midrib, clustered in groups of four or more at the ends of branches. "Echinocarpa" comes from the Latin meaning "prickly fruit." The species has a dry rather than fleshy fruit, with many spines (fig. 8), but few of the fruits mature to bear seeds.

The plant can be observed on virtually any trip to California desert areas, for it occupies desert floors, mesas, foothills, and slopes from sea level to nearly 6,000 feet from southern Mono County through Inyo County, eastern Kern County, northern Los Angeles County, and throughout the Mojave and Colorado deserts. Size, density of spines, and color of sheath vary widely, but there is no satisfactory basis for distinguishing more than one species through much of this range. In eastern Riverside and Imperial counties, however, *O. echinocarpa* mingles with *O. acanthocarpa*, but is distinguished by its shorter tubercles, shorter branches, and more erect habit. The northern Mojave Desert forms tend to be short-arborescent. Around the western upper edges of the Colorado Desert and the Borrego Valley the plants are usually more spreading, branched from the base, without a definite trunk. These bushy forms, of various spine colors, are common east of Jacumba on Highway 80.

Buckhorn Cholla; Cane Cactus
(*Opuntia acanthocarpa*)

Just as "echino" comes from the Latin and means "prickly," "acantho," from the Greek, means the same. We have two California chollas with spiny fruits

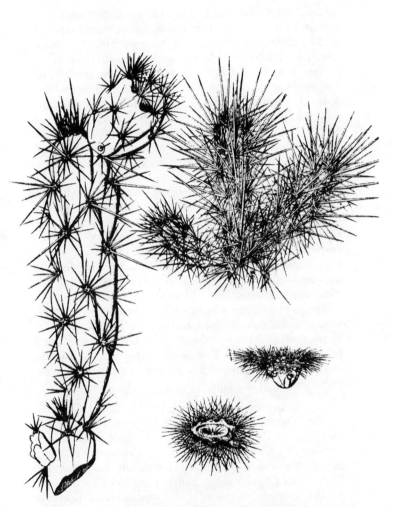

Fig. 8. *Opuntia acanthocarpa,* showing elongate tubercles of a well-watered specimen, a spiny dehydrated specimen, and spiny fruits much like those of *O. echinocarpa.*

(carpa). *Opuntia acanthocarpa* is generally more eastern and southern in distribution than *O. echinocarpa,* and is more characteristic of Arizona, although it extends well into our Mojave and Colorado deserts.

The Buckhorn Cholla is usually more bushy and outreaching than the Silver Cholla, and tends to have a much shorter or less-defined trunk when well developed. The branches are usually longer-jointed (6 to 18 inches) and the tubercules much elongated, three to four times as long as wide (fig. 8). Because of variations in both of these characters, however, distinctions are not always easy (pl. 1, *e*).

Opuntia acanthocarpa begins to mingle with *O. echinocarpa* east of Twentynine Palms and in the Chocolate Mountains east of the Salton Sea. In the vicinity of the Colorado River, however, *O. echinocarpa* fades out and *O. acanthocarpa* takes over as the only bushy cholla along our southeastern borders. It may be seen along Highway 95 north of Blythe, in the Palo Verde Mountains, and near Laguna Dam.

The name Cane Cactus refers to the use of the woody skeletons of the plant in the manufacture of canes and novelty woodcraft. The wood is hard and takes a good polish. The open lattice formed by the vascular system provides aesthetic appeal.

Valley Cholla (*Opuntia parryi*)

This is the most characteristic cylindrical *Opuntia* of the interior valleys and scrub-covered flats south and west of the deserts in southern California. It occurs more or less commonly from Cuyama Valley in Santa Barbara County, to Castaic in Los Angeles County, to Cajon Pass in San Bernardino County, and to the western edges of the Colorado and Borrego deserts. In some of our coastal areas it mingles with *O. prolifera,* and, toward the desert, with *O. echinocarpa,* but throughout much of its range west of the deserts it is the only cholla.

Opuntia parryi usually has relatively few rather long, canelike branches from the base, reaching 4 to 6 feet or more in height (pl. 2, *b*). Some plants, however, are very compactly branched and short. Others may show a densely branched arborescent habit. The joints tend to be long, for one year's growth often follows another without interruption as a joint. The branches are about an inch thick, and young ones detach easily. Since the plants tend to be rather lightly spined, the prominent tubercles show very clearly (fig. 9). The spines, brownish and inconspicuous compared with those of *O. echinocarpa*, lose their sheaths after the first season.

Fig. 9. *Opuntia parryi*, showing a young branch with prominent elongate tubercles, light spination, and fairly persistent leaves.

The inconspicuous flowers are greenish or yellowish within but reddish without. Few fruits are fertile and, unlike *O. prolifera*, these drop off the plant and do not persist to produce more flowers.

The taller forms of this species may be observed along the Santa Ana River west of Riverside, along Highway 395 in Cajon Pass, and in Castaic Canyon on Highway 99. A veritable *O. parryi* forest of small arborescent plants 3 to 5 feet tall occurs on the north side of Highway 10 just east of Cabazon. An interesting, broadly bushy, low-growing form may be seen at Banner, near Julian, on Highway 78.

Snake Cholla (*Opuntia serpentina*)

Although the Snake Cholla was one of the first cacti discovered in California, it has had a curious and confused history. First collected at San Diego (then part of Mexico) in 1838, it was provisionally named *Cereus californicus*. Later it was described in 1852 and renamed *Opuntia serpentina*, by which we still know it. For many years its rarity, local coastal distribution, and variable habit were not understood, and it was confused with other plants. During the early part of this century, collectors were unable to find it, and for some years it was considered extinct. In 1933 it was rediscovered near San Diego and brought into cultivation. We now know it as a species found in California only at Point Loma and near Chula Vista and San Ysidro, but extending southward along the Baja California coast.

Opuntia serpentina is a small cholla, usually of spreading or even prostrate habit. Some plants, however, are more or less erect. It often grows in company with *O. prolifera*, with which it apparently hybridizes to produce confusing intermediates, but plants of the two species ordinarily show very contrasting charactereristics when observed together (pl. 5, *e*).

[24]

The yellowish-green flowers are produced during April and May in a cluster near the ends of the growing branches. The fruits are dry at maturity and contain large whitish seeds.

A good place to see this plant is on a gentle slope just below the lighthouse and nature trail at Point Loma in the Cabrillo National Monument, where an excellent comparison with *O. prolifera* can be made.

Devil's Cactus (*Opuntia parishii*)

At elevations of 3,000 to 4,000 feet in the Mojave Desert at the foot of alluvial fans and on north slopes of desert ranges, occasional mats of this low, spreading cactus are seen. The stems are short, produce roots along the undersides, and grow outward from the initial point to form broad clusters and mats up to 10 feet across. The stems are almost hidden under a dense armament of angled, flattened spines an inch or more long (fig. 10). Young spines are red or pinkish, but they fade to gray at maturity, blending remarkably with the short, dry desert grass in natural camouflage. The yellow flowers appear in May and June. The fruits, about 2 inches long, are spineless but completely covered with yellow bristles (pl. 2, *c*).

This plant can be observed a few miles south of Twentynine Palms on the mesa in the Joshua Tree National Monument, and occurs in scattered patches all the way north to Clark Mountain near Highway 15. Another good place is between Cima and Goffs in northeastern San Bernardino County.

The plant was first described in the Pacific Railroad Survey report in 1856, but its present name, honoring the laborious early trips through the Mojave Desert by the San Bernardino botanist Samuel Parish, dates from 1896. It is sometimes treated as a subspecies of a more widespread Arizona species, *O. stanlyi*.

In easternmost Imperial County occurs a much

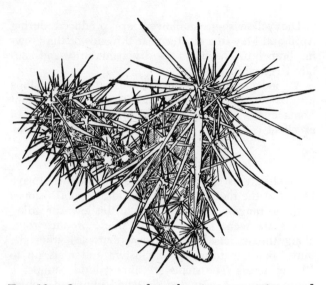

Fig. 10. *Opuntia parishii,* showing two joints and flattened spines.

larger form of the Devil's Cactus, *Opuntia wrightiana,* with stems 4 to 8 inches long and 1 to 1½ inches in diameter (fig. 11). It is sometimes treated as a subspecies in the *O. stanlyi* complex comparable with *O. parishii.* The plant may be found on the flats southwest of Winterhaven, near Yuma.

Dwarf Cholla (*Opuntia pulchella*)

The Dwarf Cholla is one of a group of inconspicuous small chollas (sometimes known as *Micropuntia*) characterized by large tuberous underground stems and very short, clustered, aboveground stems only 1 to 4 inches high (fig. 12). The plants occur in areas in which cacti are unexpected and, being exceedingly small and inconspicuous in the grass, are seldom seen except when the relatively large purple flowers (1 to 1½ inches) are open. The range is from northern

Arizona and southwestern Utah across southern Nevada to the edge of California in Mono County in the vicinity of the White Mountains and probably the Walker River.

Fig. 11. *Opuntia wrightiana,* showing joints and bristle-covered fruit.

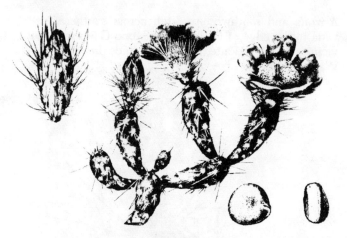

Fig. 12. *Opuntia pulchella*, showing part of a flowering plant, a spiny bud, and two seeds.

PLATYOPUNTIA: THE PRICKLY PEARS

The prickly pears are the most tolerant and widespread of all cacti and occur in the greatest number of species (more than 200). They comprise the one group that ranges in California from farthest north to farthest south. In their principal homeland, Mexico, they have been used since the ancient times of the Toltecs and Aztecs. The fruits and the tender young pads have long been common foods (tunas and nopales). The plants are widely cultivated for hedges. The juice is employed medicinally for burns, as a laxative, and in the treatment of diabetes. In California the prickly pear received great notoriety as a result of Luther Burbank's development of spineless cacti. In some countries, particularly Australia, introduced opuntias were once serious pests and, before controls were developed, spread over millions of acres.

[28]

The California prickly pears are the most difficult of our cacti to identify because of their great variation and extensive intergradation. Much of this is due to the ability of the natural species to hybridize with one another and with the two principal forms of cacti introduced from Mexico 200 years ago by the mission founders along El Camino Real.

Beaver Tail Cactus (*Opuntia basilaris*)
(Illustrated on front cover)

The Beaver Tail Cactus, a widespread *Opuntia* of our deserts and mountains, bears some of the loveliest flowers of any of our native plants. These cacti occur in a diversity of habitats and show a wide range of forms.

Typical *Opuntia basilaris* is a low-growing plant consisting of several flat, obovate pads, 5 to 10 inches long, arising from a common base. The pads are greenish to purplish, often transversely wrinkled, and apparently spineless (fig. 13). They suggest the shape of a beaver's tail. Although the areoles bear no obvious spines, they are filled with packs of glochids which can cause great misery if they get on one's clothing and then into the skin. From March to June in various parts of our deserts this plant produces magnificent cluster of rose- to orchid-colored flowers up to 3 inches across. The fruits are dry when ripe and contain whitish seeds. This is one of the succulent plants widely used in ancient times by the desert Indians, such as the Panamint tribe. All parts were used for food: pads, flower buds, young fruits, and seeds.

Opuntia basilaris in its typical form may be found throughout much of the Mojave, Colorado, and Borrego deserts from nearly 6,000 feet to about sea level. It may be seen upon entering the desert by highways 10, 15, 74, 80, and 78, and throughout much of the

[29]

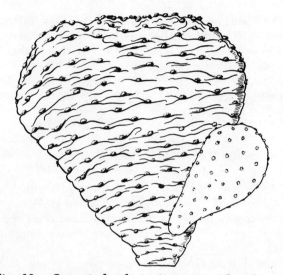

Fig. 13. *Opuntia basilaris*. A young pad and an old, wrinkled pad.

Joshua Tree National Monument and the Anza-Borrego Desert State Park.

A number of interesting forms of *O. basilaris* occur other than the typical one. In Kern County east of Bakersfield is the variety *treleasii*, best seen on either side of Walker Pass. It is marked by the presence of spines in the areoles in addition to the glochids. Along the east slope of the Sierra Nevada in Inyo and Mono counties at elevations up to 9,000 feet (such as the middle slopes of Mount Whitney), is a dwarfish, pink-flowered form, sometimes with white flowers, known as variety *whitneyana*. On desert slopes of the San Gabriel and San Bernardino mountains may be found the variety *brachyclada*, with very narrow, short, thick, and fingerlike pads. In the interior valleys of coastal drainage in southern California, especially trom San Bernardino to Claremont, occurs a form in which the pads are branched in upper parts instead of only at the base. This is the variety *ramosa* (pl. 5, *d*). Each of these major variants has been treated by some students of cacti as a separate species. They do tend to maintain their distinctive characteristics in cultivation.

Opuntia basilaris var. *brachyclada* has been called the Snow Flower Cactus, for it comes into brilliant flower soon after melting of the snow that covers the plant in winter. It grows under piñon pines and mountain shrubs at elevations of 4,000 to 7,500 feet around Wrightwood and in Swartout Valley.

Old Man Prickly Pear; Grizzly Bear Cactus
(*Opuntia erinacea*)

Opuntia erinacea has a low-growing, clumping habit similar to that of *O. basilaris*, but the pads are covered with grayish, whitish, or even blackish spines of varying length. In the form known as *O. erinacea* var. *ursina*, the white spines are so long and soft as to cover the plant with a kind of white hair (pl. 2, *d*). These hairy plants are popular as novelty specimens in gardens, and wild populations are rapidly being reduced by plant hunters. At the other extreme is the variety *xanthostema* in which the spines are sparse, short, and mostly absent from the lower half of the joints. The flowers of these diverse forms of *O. erinacea* are prevailingly yellow, but vary to pink and reddish. The fruits are dry and short-spiny.

Typical *O. erinacea*, which has abundant rigid spines 1 to 2 inches or more long (pl. 2, *e*), is a plant of moderate elevations (2,500 to 8,000 feet) in the western Mojave Desert from the San Bernardino Mountains through Inyo County to Mono County. A fine stand occurs in Wild Rose Canyon near the entrance to Death Valley. A far southern colony lives in the Santa Rosa Mountains of Riverside County.

[31]

The long-haired variety *ursina* occurs in the central and eastern Mojave Desert at elevations of 3,000 to 4,500 feet. It was discovered in 1894 by A. H. Alverson of San Bernardino, a cactus enthusiast who operated a prospector's supply outpost. When he learned from a desert gold seeker of the existence of a cactus with white hair a foot long, he organized a horse-and-wagon party to find it. The party suffered great hardships on the desert for lack of water, but found the plant in the Ord Mountains and introduced it to the horticultural world. It may be seen there today, where it is regenerating after suffering near-extinction at the hands of commercial collectors two decades ago.

The lightly spined variety *xanthostema* has a remarkable distribution for a cactus. It is a high-elevation form that survives heavy snow cover. It grows on desert slopes of the Sierra Nevada and the White Mountains as high as 11,000 feet. A visitor to Convict Lake in Mono County will find it on sandy exposures around the east end of the lake.

Golden Prickly Pear; Pancake Pear
(*Opuntia chlorotica*)
(Illustrated on front cover)

Opuntia chlorotica is one of our few distinctive large prickly pears. A striking plant when well developed, it has bright yellow spines and a prominent treelike habit with definite trunk often covered with a thatch of long spines. The yellow flowers show little contrast with the spines, but the fruits are bright red or purplish. The plant reaches a height of 6 or more feet, and has such well-rounded pads that it is referred to as Pancake Pear (pl. 2, *f*; fig. 14).

Although it is prominent and easily recognized, the plant is not often seen in California, for its habitats here are scattered and mostly not readily accessible.

[32]

a. Opuntia ramosissima

b. Opuntia bigelovii

c. Opuntia bigelovii

d. Opuntia acanthocarpa

e. Opuntia acanthocarpa

f. Opuntia echinocarpa

PLATE 1

a. Opuntia prolifera   *b. Opuntia parryi*

c. Opuntia parishii   *d. Opuntia ursina*

e. Opuntia erinacea   *f. Opuntia chlorotica*

PLATE 2

a. Opuntia ficus-indica   *b. Opuntia megacantha*

c. Opuntia oricola (l.);   *d. Opuntia littoralis*
Opuntia littoralis (r.)

e, f. Opuntia vaseyi (red); *Opuntia covillei* (yellow)

PLATE 3

a. Opuntia piercei　　　*b. Opuntia piercei*

c. Opuntia occidentalis　　*d. Opuntia occidentalis*

f. Opuntia megacarpa

e. Opuntia oricola

PLATE 4

a. Bergerocactus emoryi

b. Echinocereus engelmannii

c. Ferocactus covillei

d. Opuntia basilaris var. *ramosa*

e. Opuntia prolifera (erect); *Opuntia serpentina* (low).

PLATE 5

a. Carnegiea gigantea *b. Carnegiea gigantea*

c. Echinocereus boyce-thompsonii *d. Echinomastus johnsonii*

e. Echinocereus engelmannii *f. Echinocereus mojavensis*

PLATE 6

a. Echinocactus polycephalus *b. Echinocactus polycephalus*

c. Ferocactus acanthodes *d. Ferocactus acanthodes*

e. Ferocactus viridescens *f. Sclerocactus polyancistrus*

PLATE 7

a. Coryphantha deserti   *b. Coryphantha alversonii*

c. Coryphantha alversonii   *d. Coryphantha arizonica*

e. Mammillaria dioica   *f. Phellosperma tetrancistra*

PLATE 8

Fig. 14. *Opuntia chlorotica,* showing a single round pad.

Abundant growths occur in Arizona, New Mexico, and Sonora, Mexico. Perhaps the best place to see *O. chlorotica* conveniently is in Sentenac Canyon on Highway 78 below Julian, where many specimens stand on the steep south walls of the gorge below Scissors Crossing. On Highway 80 it occurs 3.3 miles east of Pine Valley and along the Mexican boundary fence 3 miles east of Jacumba. It is more widely distributed throughout the eastern half of San Bernardino County, where it grows in mountainous areas and on desert plateaus at about 4,000 feet. Some large plants occur in the Joshua Tree National Monument, and fine stands may be seen between Goffs and Cima in the Providence Mountains region.

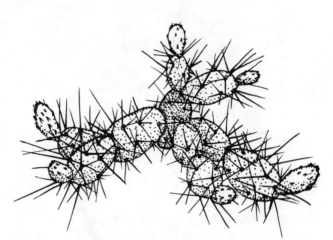

Fig. 15. *Opuntia fragilis.* Habit of part of a plant.

Pigmy Tuna (*Opuntia fragilis*)

This small prickly pear is one of the few cacti adapted to life in the severe climate of interior continental America. It grows as far north as Manitoba, Canada, and survives heavy winter snows and temperatures as low as 50° below zero. It is characteristic of the Great Plains, forming low, spreading clusters and mounds 1 to 4 feet in diameter, but mostly hidden in grass. It has been a troublesome weed in grazing country because of the small, thick, spiny joints which become detached at the slightest touch and fasten into the flesh of the nose and lips of range animals (fig. 15).

The plant is widely distributed in arid parts of the Northwest between southern British Columbia and northern California. We find it in Siskiyou County in dry places in the juniper country. It flowers in May and June, but the pale yellow flowers are sparse and seldom seen.

[34]

Indian Fig (*Opuntia ficus-indica*)

This large, shrubby to treelike, nearly spineless cactus probably had its origins in prehistoric times in tropical America. Most likely it was developed in the Mexican region and was already widely cultivated, mainly for its fruits (fig. 16), when the Spaniards arrived. It was soon transplanted to Europe, north Africa, and other regions where it became naturalized. Large plantations were established in the Mediterranean area. One of the most important agricultural crops of Sicily has long been *Opuntia* fruits, of which some 18,000 pounds per acre can be harvested (pl. 3, *a*).

The Indian Fig, introduced into southern California from Mexico as one of the mission cacti, has spread with *O. megacantha* throughout much of the cismontane part of the state. Similarity with the spiny *O.*

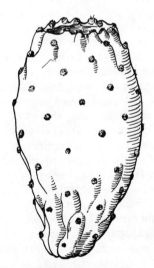

Fig. 16. *Opuntia ficus-indica*, fruit.

megacantha and occasional reversions of the spineless form to spiny ones strongly suggest the origin of this plant from *O. megacantha*. Both plants hybridize freely with each other and with several of the native California prickly pears.

Large treelike examples of this plant with smooth, elongate, nearly spineless pads may be seen near each of the old California missions along El Camino Real from San Diego to San Francisco Bay. A commercial row-planting occurs on the east side of Highway 101 about 3 miles south of Coyote, near San Jose.

Mission Cactus (*Opuntia megacantha*)

From the Mission Cactus the best varieties of edible fruits are obtained. It is similar to *Opuntia ficus-indica*, but has more rounded pads and fairly abundant coarse spines. It forms similar large treelike plants which in age develop heavy trunks. The flowers, yellow to yellow-orange, are producd mostly in May and June. The large yellowish to reddish fruits (pl. 3, *b*) mature in November and December They are spineless, but have many glochids which must be brushed off carefully before the fruit is handled.

Opuntia megacantha came into California two hundred years ago at Mission San Diego de Alcalá. Pieces subsequently planted along the old Mexican trails hybridized widely with several species of prickly pears. The resulting hybrid swarm of variations has made it increasingly difficult to identify the several natural species from Santa Barbara to San Bernardino and San Diego, whose natural distributions and characteristics are unknown to us. Within a single prickly pear thicket one may find plants showing a wide range of characters linking them in varying degrees to one or several of the named species treated below.

Like the Indian Fig, the Mission Cactus may be seen in clearly recognizable typical form around the Spanish mission communities along El Camino Real, but there are numerous confusing intergrades as well. One of the largest stands occurs at La Purisima Mission near Lompoc.

An important unnamed hybrid form, probably involving *O. covillei*, occurs from Claremont to Murrieta and east of the Santa Ana Mountains. It is a shorter, more shrubby form than typical *O. megacantha* and has weak spination. The flowers are larger and more rotate. The fruits are reddish-purple, oblong and basally tapered.

Short Coastal Prickly Pear (*Opuntia littoralis*)

Opuntia littoralis has long been considered the principal prickly pear along coastal southern California from Santa Barbara to San Diego and southward, usually within about 5 miles of the coast, but occasionally inland at low elevations and also on the Channel Islands. Recently it has been determined that more than one species is involved throughout this range. Besides *O. littoralis* and the recently described *O. oricola*, other kinds of fleshy-fruited prickly pears grow in relatively restricted areas along the southern California coast, but since these remain unnamed, we shall not consider them here.

Opuntia littoralis is a more spreading plant than *O. oricola*, seldom erect, and usually less than 4 feet tall. Besides their habit of growth, the two species exhibit several other conspicuous differences. The pads of *O. littoralis* are more oblong-elliptical, and the spines are usually straight (pl. 3, *c*). The color of unweathered spines is bone white rather than clear, translucent yellowish. The fruits have an obpyriform rather than globular shape (pl. 3, *d*). The morphological characters of *O. littoralis* are somewhat more varied than those of the clearly defined *O. oricola*.

Both species may be met within nearly every coastal and insular prickly pear colony. Some good places to see and compare them are along Highway 101 entering the Conejo Mountains east of Camarillo, on the sea cliffs near Malibu Beach, along the seaward Palos Verdes Hills, on the coast north of Laguna Beach at Irvine Cove, at Dana Point Cove off Green Lantern Street, and in the Cabrillo National Monument at San Diego.

Fig. 17. *Opuntia oricola,* flower in longitudinal section.

Tall Coast Prickly Pear (*Opuntia oricola*)

This newly described plant (1964) has long been confused with *Opuntia littoralis,* which has virtually the same range. When one learns the distinctions between the two, however, he can recognize each from a distance. *Opuntia oricola* is usually of erect rather than spreading habit; mature plants are often 6 feet or more tall. The pads are almost circular in outline rather than oblong-elliptical as in *O. littoralis.* Rather than bone white, the spines are a clear, translucent yellow in unweathered condition. Flowers are yellow as in *O. littoralis* (fig. 17). The fruits tend to be globular rather than elongate, and lack the narrowed base of *O. littoralis.* Although some of the spines are straight, and occasionally all may be nearly straight, the heavier spines are often characterized by a prominent downward curvature (pls. 3, *c*, 4, *e*).

These large plants can usually be spotted in colonies of coastal prickly pears by their round pads. Look for

[38]

them in *Opuntia* thickets in the coastal sage vegetation all the way from San Diego to Santa Barbara and a few miles inland. Besides the several near-coastal localities mentioned under *O. littoralis,* a fine stand occurs on north Euclid Avenue in Fullerton. A few large specimens may be seen along Foothill Road near the Santa Barbara Botanic Garden, growing with *O. megacantha.*

Another coastal and near-coastal plant ranging from central Orange County to near San Diego and inland about 20 miles is an undescribed form showing some characteristics of *O. littoralis, O. occidentalis,* and *O. megacantha.* The pads are large, with widely spaced areoles, long yellow to yellow-brown spines, large rotate flowers, and large and persistent leaves.

Western Prickly Pear (*Opuntia occidentalis*)

There is much confusion over just what *Opuntia occidentalis* really is, although the name is widely used in floras and, indeed, various other plants are assigned to it as varieties or subspecies. The plant generally known under this name occupies a territory throughout most of Orange County and inland to the foothills of the San Gabriel Mountains. We recognize it as a large bushy plant reaching about 6 feet in height. It bears moderately heavy brown spines, with lighter golden tips, 1 to 1½ inches long and tending to be deflexed. A distinctive character is. the long awl-shaped leaf on young pads, sometimes longer than half an inch. The flowers are yellowish to cream. The ovary is markedly tuberculate and has persistent leaves. The style is bulbous. Fruits are red to somewhat maroon and moderately large, about 2½ by 1¾ inches (pl. 4, c).

These plants may be found associated with *Opuntia vaseyi* and *O. covillei* in inland areas, and with *O.*

littoralis and *O. oricola* nearer the coast. They show evidence of being a hybrid between the Mission Cactus and *Opuntia vaseyi*.

Localities in which to observe characteristic plants of *O. occidentalis* are in the vicinity of Fullerton, especially at Yorba Linda and Placentia.

Salmon-flowered Prickly Pear (*Opuntia vaseyi*)

Opuntia vaseyi is a low-growing plant only 1 to 1½ feet tall and spreading to 8 to 10 feet, but with brown, golden-tipped spines similar to those of the more erect *O. occidentalis*. The flowers are distinctive in being deep salmon-colored, for this is the only one of our larger spiny prickly pears with such flowers (pl. 3, *e*).

The range is restricted to the inland valleys from about Buena Park north to San Dimas, east to Banning, and south to Hemet. There are no known coastal localities.

Opuntia vaseyi has been treated in some floras as a variety of *O. occidentalis*, but it is evidently an ancestral California type not modified by hybridization. It shows some vegetative variation in the direction of *O. piercei*, but not in flower color.

Good places to see this plant are along the foothills of the San Gabriel Mountains by State Highway 30 northeast of Upland.

Coville's Prickly Pear (*Opuntia covillei*)

Opuntia covillei is another variable prickly pear whose specific limits can scarcely be defined and whose identification cannot always clearly be made. It is a low-growing plant similar in habit to *O. vaseyi*, but with lemon-yellow flowers tinged with red on the outer perianth segments (pl. 3, *e*). Some plants may be bushy and up to 3 feet tall. The pads are more variable in shape than in *O. vaseyi*, and the spines, which are commonly twisted, are typically restricted to the upper half of the pad. The fruits are a dull purplish red.

Opuntia covillei represents a major segment of the hybrid swarm of prickly pears from the interior valleys of southern California. Some characters suggest relationship with the Mission Cactus and with *O. megacarpa*. Other characters suggest partial derivation, together with *O. vaseyi* and *O. piercei* of this same complex, from the widespread, more eastern *O. phaeacantha* common in Arizona. *Opuntia covillei* has been treated as a variety of *O. phaeacantha* and also as a variety of *O. occidentalis*.

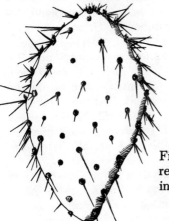

Fig. 18. An *Opuntia* pad representing one form within the *O. covillei* complex.

This variable assemblage now occupies a region encompassing Orange County and extending to the foothills of the San Gabriel and San Bernardino mountains. Toward the coast the distinction from *O. littoralis* becomes confused as the spination spreads over the entire pads.

Perhaps the most representative forms of this plant may be seen along State Highway 30 northeast of Upland, where it contrasts with the salmon-flowered *O. vaseyi* (pl. 3, *e*). It is part of the big hybrid mass of prickly pears conspicuous along the San Bernardino freeway just west of Pomona near the fairgrounds.

Banning Prickly Pear (*Opuntia megacarpa*)

Opuntia megacarpa, originally described from specimens collected at Banning, is distributed on dry mountain slopes around the western and southern edges of our deserts. The species shows relationship with two more easterly species in Arizona: *O. phaeacantha* and *O. engelmannii*. It has large pads and the plants are erect but short, not as decumbent as *O. piercei*, which often grows in the same area and with which it seems to merge and hybridize in San Diego County (pl. 4, *f*). The white and yellow spines, 2 inches or more long, tend to be twisted and not much downwardly deflected. They are rather uniformly distributed over the stem joints, whereas those of *O. piercei* are usually confined to the upper half. Glochids are conspicuous. The fruits are not necessarily or especially large, despite the name.

The range may be outlined as from Riverside and the east side of the Santa Ana Mountains, to the north side of Palomar Mountain, northeast to the desert slopes of the Santa Rosa and San Jacinto mountains, to the southern desert edges of the San Bernardino Mountains. Along the mountain slopes bordering the Anza-Borrego Desert *O. megacarpa* merges with *O. piercei*, and evident hybrid forms may be encountered.

Typical plants may be observed around Banning, and upgrade toward Redlands. A good stand grows in the vicinity of Lake Mathews.

Pierce's Prostrate Prickly Pear (*Opuntia piercei*)

Another plant related to the Arizona *Opuntia phaea-*

cantha, and originally described as a variety of it, is *O. piercei* from our desert mountain slopes at 3,000 to 7,000 feet. These remarkably prostrate plants form "creeping clumps" in which the joints root down successively at one end as they grow out one on another, and die back at the other end. The spines are 2 to 3 inches long and usually single from each areole in the upper half of the nearly circular pads. The flowers are yellow and the fruits red to dull purplish and slender (pl. 4, *a*).

This plant has a montane range on the desert sides of the San Gabriel, San Bernardino, Santa Rosa, and Laguna mountains. It occurs in areas receiving rather heavy winter snow. Some good places to observe *O. piercei* are above Baldwin Lake in the San Bernardino Mountains, at Warner's Hot Springs in San Diego County, along Highway 79 in the Cuyamaca Mountains, and along Highway 94 just east of Jacumba.

Mojave Desert Prickly Pear (*Opuntia mojavensis*)

The large-padded prickly pears of the California deserts have not been studied adequately, and we do not have a clear understanding of the relationship of

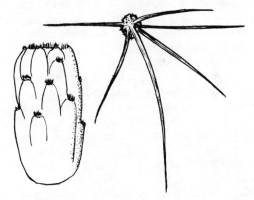

Fig. 19. *Opuntia mojavensis.* A young, spineless fruit and a spine cluster removed from a pad.

some of our forms to those eastward into Arizona and Nevada. *Opuntia mojavensis* evidently is closely related to *O. phaeacantha* and *O. engelmannii* in Arizona. It was described from the Providence Mountains area and is presently known from the eastern Mojave Desert north to the Clark Mountains. Some of the desert prickly pears in the Anza-Borrego Desert area seem closely related to *O. mojavensis* and to *O. engelmannii,* but have not been sufficiently investigated.

Opuntia mojavensis is a primarily prostrate plant in which the secondary pads are erect, but the whole plant is only about 1½ feet high. The joints are large (8 to 12 inches) and bear yellowish-brown, porrect spines up to 2½ inches long (fig. 19). The flowers are pale yellow to orange. The fruits are spineless, slender, and narrow at the base when mature.

Published localities for *O. mojavensis* include the vicinity of the Bonanza King mine in the Providence Mountains and the region adjoining Highway 95 on the California side of the Nevada state boundary.

Giant Cactus; Saguaro (*Carnegiea gigantea*)

So abundant and prevalent throughout Arizona is this magnificent succulent that it is often called the Arizona Giant Cactus. Indeed, near Tucson the Saguaro National Monument has been set up exclusively for it. Nevertheless, this plant occurs also in California, although not extensively or in large numbers (pl. 6, *a*). A few scattered specimens are found near the Colorado River from the Palo Verde Mountains southward toward Laguna Dam, near which a fairly large grove occurs. Another large stand is in the Whipple Mountains near the Parker Dam and reservoir. Thirty years ago, before Parker Lake was formed, it was known that many of the giant cacti would be flooded out by rising water, and permits were issued to cactus enthusiasts who wanted to transplant them. The writer, then in high school, was one of these, and it was to my extraordinary delight that my father agreed to help me bring one home as the biggest cactus in town. It was a 22-foot giant with two limbs, and required considerable engineering to get it home to Long Beach and plant it in the back yard. There it lived and flowered for many years before it finally succumbed to rot.

The saguaro is the northernmost of the giant columnar cacti of which a number of species and genera occur in Mexico and a few in South America. This species probably should be treated under one of the Mexican genera, but it has long honored Andrew Carnegie, the benefactor of Britton and Rose, who monographed the Cactaceae early in this century and dedicated the largest American cactus to him.

The giant cactus for centuries served the Indians of the Southwest with food, fuel, and building material. The season of ripe fruits brought whole tribal populations into the cactus forest for feasting and the preparation of dried fruits for winter use. One frugal tribe of the desert even saved the seeds from their own feces to be ground up and eaten a second time.

The huge fleshy stem is supported by a woody cylinder consisting of a ring of anastomosing poles of great strength. This strong internal skeleton accounts for the size of these plants, which may reach 60 feet. Flowering is in May and June (pl. 6, *b*).

Velvet Cactus (*Bergerocactus emoryi*)

In 1850 the United States and Mexican Boundary Survey party discovered this plant where the first international boundary marker was installed south of Imperial Beach in San Diego County. It still may be found there, although elsewhere in southern California *Bergerocactus* has largely been exterminated by our urban sprawl along the coast. As late as 1930 it could still be found at Oceanside and San Clemente, but only a few patches now remain around San Diego.

The best one is protected by the Cabrillo National Monument and is marked on its nature trail just below the lighthouse. It can be seen there in its characteristic habit, producing pale yellow flowers in spring, and fruits in late summer. The globular, spiny red fruits are peculiar in the manner in which they split open at maturity and allow the red pulp and black seeds to ooze out.

Bergerocactus is a seacoast plant that extends far south into Baja California. It is abundant on San Clemente Island and occurs to some extent on Santa Catalina. It forms thickets of erect or sprawling plants, 2 to 3 feet long or high, which multiply by sending out branches from below the surface of the ground. New stems have bright yellow spines which fade and darken with age (pl. 5, *a*).

This plant is often treated in western floras as *Cereus emoryi*. A number of characteristics make it unique, however, and when segregated from *Cereus* it remains the only member of this genus named for the German botanist Alwin Berger. In Baja California it is known to form natural hybrids with the large candelabra cactus (*Myrtillocactus*) and with the giant cardon (*Pachycereus*). The results are some very rare and peculiar cacti that are known only from one or a very few specimens (*Myrtgerocactus* and *Pachgerocereus*).

Hedgehog Cactus; Strawberry Cactus
(*Echinocereus engelmannii*)

The brilliantly colored magenta to purplish flowers of the Hedgehog Cactus make it a popular subject for illustrations of desert wildflowers (pl. 5, *b*). Moreover, the species is one of the most abundant of the freely flowering kinds in arid regions close to population centers in southern California. It is an exceedingly spiny plant made up of several to many elongate heads

[46]

loosely arranged in a clump, the 2-to-3-inch spines interlacing the spaces between (pl. 6, *e*).

The flowers of hedgehog cacti are fairly long-lasting, opening each of several mornings and closing at night. They vary in color, but tend to have bluish tones from pigment mixtures unlike those of *E. mojavensis*, in which only red pigment occurs. The common name Strawberry Cactus refers to the succulent, edible red fruits which drop their spines when ripe.

Echinocereus engelmannii has a wide range in California, from nearly sea level in the Colorado Desert to elevations of 7,000 feet on dry slopes. It extends north through the Mojave Desert to the White Mountains and on into Arizona. The species may be observed throughout much of the Joshua Tree National Monument and the Anza-Borrego Desert State Park. One of the most abundant stands is on the hills along Highway 80 just east of Jacumba, where the plants are spaced only a few feet apart.

Some authors recognize *E. munzii* as a separate species; this plant, which is at least very closely related, occurs in mountain areas in Riverside, San Bernardino, and San Diego counties at the lower edge of the yellow-pine forest and into the piñon-juniper woodlands. It tends to form very compact clumps of numerous stems. It may be seen above Baldwin Lake on the desert slopes of the San Bernardino Mountains.

Mound Cactus; Mojave Hedgehog Cactus
(*Echinocereus mojavensis*)

Adult plants of this species form massive hemispherical mounds several feet in diameter, composed of enormous numbers of densely-packed spiny stems radiating from a common center. Plants with 500 to 800 of these heads have been reported. The spines, white or gray, are 1 to 2 inches long. The deep scarlet color of the flowers is striking in contrast to the pale spines (pl. 6, *f*). They appear around Easter time.

[47]

This remarkable plant was discovered more than a hundred years ago as a result of explorations for the route of the Pacific Railway. It was first illustrated in 1856. We now know it to occur widely but not very abundantly throughout mountain ranges of the Mojave Desert from the desert slopes of the San Bernardino range northeast to Clark Mountain and on through Death Valley National Monument to the White Mountains. It may be found in association with Creosote Bush, Joshua Tree, or Piñon Pine and Juniper, but it is a plant of rocky slopes at elevations of 3,000 to 7,000 feet and not of desert floors. It may be seen in the Joshua Tree National Monument associated with *Opuntia parishii*, a few miles south of Twenty-nine Palms on the mesa at Lost Horse Well, and around Mitchell's Caverns in the Providence Mountains.

Some workers consider this plant a variant of *Echinocereus triglochidiatus*, a species of broad distribution and great variability eastward through Arizona, New Mexico, and Texas. However, in California it is markedly distinct from any other cactus, particularly when in flower.

Boyce Thompson Hedgehog Cactus
(*Echinocereus boyce-thompsonii*)

The Clark Mountain area north of Valley Wells in far northeastern San Bernardino County is a California outpost for this plant characteristically found in central Arizona. It is generally treated as a sub-specific variant within the *Echinocereus fendleri* complex, which includes diverse plants through Arizona, New Mexico, and Sonora. This one resembles *E. engelmannii* superficially in its rather open clusters of several elongate fleshy stems, but is distinct in having only a single prominent, deflexed central spine from each areole. These long central spines are distinctly light-colored and contrast with the dark radials (pl. 6, *c*). The flowers, magenta to purplish, are 2 to 2¾ inches in diameter.

[48]

Desert Barrel Cactus (*Ferocactus acanthodes*)

This legendary plant is supposed to have saved many a desert traveler from death by thirst. To be sure, it has a succulent pulp from which life-sustaining though unpleasant moisture can be obtained by crushing or chewing the flesh, but it is not cool, clear liquid water. In recent decades this succulent flesh, not unlike watermelon rind, has been employed in making cactus candy and pickles, although the plants are now protected by law against such use.

The Desert Barrel Cactus is easy to recognize, but variations in size, shape, and color have led botanists in the past to see several species in the assemblage. The commonest form is heavy-bodied and short, usually less than 3 feet tall and a foot or more in diameter. It occurs on most rocky slopes leading to the Borrego and Colorado deserts (pl. 7, *c*). In southeasternmost Imperial County are some very tall forms that may exceed 8 feet. The spines are generally yellow or straw-colored, but some examples have bright red spines and others have gray or white spines. All these are now considered variants of the single species. The yellow flowers often present a colorful corona (pl. 7, *d*).

Most plants have solitary heads, but clusters of two or three are sometimes seen. These are usually separate plants growing close together, since the barrel cacti infrequently branch. Growth is very slow, and may occur only at long intervals. In fact, these plants, with their reserve water supply, can live and flower year after year sitting on a dry shelf in the sun.

Ferocactus acanthodes ranges through the Borrego and Colorado deserts and the middle and eastern Mojave Desert below 5,000 feet, and on into Arizona, Nevada, and Baja California. Good stands may be observed at Split Rock in the Joshua Tree National Monument, in the Devil's Playground area south of

Baker, in Sentenac Canyon below Julian, and on the Mountain Springs grade west of El Centro. A fine display occurs on the north side of Highway 10 just below Whitewater, near Palm Springs.

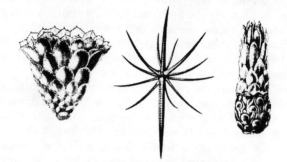

Fig. 20. *Ferocactus viridescens*, showing flower, fruit, and spine cluster.

Coast Barrel Cactus (*Ferocactus viridescens*)

This species of "fierce" cactus is so small and low that it scarcely suggests the barrel form of its near relative *Ferocactus acanthodes*. It is distinct, too, in habitat, for it is strictly a coastal species of San Diego County and northern Baja California, seldom occurring more than 20 miles from the shore. It lives in the chaparral north to about Escondido and is especially common in the Cabrillo National Monument at Point Loma, San Diego, where it can be observed conveniently on the nature trail. Some of the finest and largest plants occur on Otay Mesa a few miles southeast. The specimens usually form single heads, but clusters of several are not uncommon.

The name "viridescens" refers to the greenish flowers which appear in spring (fig. 20), followed by spineless yellow fruits (pl. 7, *e*), which contain quantities of black seeds easily removed at maturity. These

[50]

were among the common food seeds of the San Diego Indians before Spanish grains were brought to California.

This is a good plant in which to observe protective armament, for the spination has developed remarkably complete protection against herbivores. The central spines are exceedingly strong and so symmetrically arranged as to fend off deer or rabbits from any direction. The radial spines form a protective mesh over the succulent ribs and are so securely fastened that they can scarcely be removed even by a pawing hoof (fig. 20).

Coville's Barrel Cactus (*Ferocactus covillei*)

Not long ago some amateur cactus hunters brought into my office a young specimen of a barrel cactus that they had never before found in California. Although juvenile, this plant seemed to have all the characters of *Ferocactus covillei*, particularly the single heavy, hooked central spine and the small number of strong radials. It was said to have come from a canyon along the Mexican boundary a few miles east of Jacumba in southwesternmost Imperial County. The known range of this species otherwise is about 200 miles farther east in Arizona (pl. 5, *c*).

Nigger Heads (*Echinocactus polycephalus*)

The old genus *Echinocactus* of nineteenth-century authors contains over a thousand names, and embraces a great diversity of cactus species of globular form. Britton and Rose, in volume 3 of their monograph on the Cactaceae in 1922, recognized a number of distinctive genera within the assemblage and restricted *Echinocactus* to a small group of barrel cacti with dense wool at the top of the plant. Some manuals, however, continue to use *Echinocactus* in the old inclusive sense.

[51]

Most species of *Echinocactus* are ponderous, single-headed giants from central Mexico, but, as the name indicates, *E. polycephalus* is a many-headed form. Plants with 10 to 20 heads are common, and an enormous specimen of 132 heads grew near Yermo until it was hacked to pieces by vandals (pl. 7, *a*).

Except for very young plants, this species is immediately distinguished from *Ferocactus acanthodes* by its multiheaded character. The yellow flowers are borne in the woolly crown. The fruits are densely woolly (fig. 21), dry at maturity, and open by a basal pore.

Echinocactus polycephalus is a plant of the most forbidding, hot, dry desert mountains, from northern Inyo County and the Panamints beside Death Valley to Randsburg and Victorville in the Mojave Desert, and on east into Arizona. A small outlying colony occurs in the Coyote Mountains of Imperial County. The species can be observed in characteristic habitat around Barstow and Calico Ghost Town off Highway 15. Some fine stands occur around Scotty's Castle in Death Valley.

Fig. 21. *Echinocactus polycephalus*, fruit.

Pigmy Barrel Cactus (*Echinomastus johnsonii*)

This distinctive small barrel cactus is seldom seen in California on account of the remoteness of its habitat in the far northeastern Mojave Desert, north of the Kingston range in the east corner of Inyo County, and east of the Ivanpah Mountains. It is occasional there on dry rocky slopes and washes, a small, solitary barrel cactus 5 to 10 inches high. It consists of 18 to 20 spiral ribs fairly well marked into tubercles and provided with dense, coarse, nearly straight spines.

The plant generally appears in floras as *Echinocactus johnsonii* and has also been treated as a species of *Ferocactus*. Specialists in recent years have considered the small size, the low ribs with felted grooves, and the short-tubed flowers as characters of the genus *Echinomastus*, which includes similar species in Utah and Arizona.

The flowers appear in groups and protrude from between the spines at the apex (pl. 6, *d*). They are of variable color, from deep red and brownish to pink, salmon, apricot, and even white. In one Nevada form they are lemon yellow. They have the unusual capacity of opening and closing for as many as seven successive days.

This plant may be observed in sparse colonies in the hills in the vicinity of Shoshone along Highway 127 east of Death Valley and in the New York Mountains near Ivanpah.

Long-spined Fishhook Cactus
(*Sclerocactus polyancistrus*)

The magnificent spiny beauty of this colorful succulent is leading to its extinction in all desert areas frequented by man. The plant is solitary, unbranched, 8 to 12 inches tall, and covered with long white and maroon spines of which the longest colored ones are strongly hooked (fig. 22). So rare and peculiar is the plant that anyone finding it in the desert is inclined

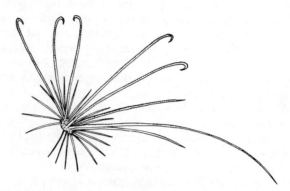

Fig. 22. *Sclerocactus polyancistrus* spine cluster.

to dig it up and take it home. This is the end of the cactus, for *Sclerocactus* does not live well or long in cultivation, often because of rot that forms in the passages made by a boring grub in the fleshy tissues of this species. In nature the plant seals off the wounds and survives, but not in captivity.

The flowers are magenta, from the apex (pl. 7, *f*), and the fruits are smooth and red.

Several widely scattered areas of the Mojave Desert in which this rare plant grows have been searched so thoroughly by cactus hunters that few specimens may now be found within easy access of roads. Nevertheless, a good desert hiker may luckily find this prized species in the Roaring Ridge area of Red Rock Canyon, or between Adelanto, Oro Grande, and Helendale west of Highway 15. (These are also the homelands of the desert tortoise.) Very large specimens occur in the Opal Mountain area north of Barstow.

Desert Pincushion Cactus (*Coryphantha deserti*)

The California coryphanthas comprise a group of small, single- or multi-headed cacti which can be distinguished from our mammillarias by the straight spines and by a groove on the upper side of the tubercles. We have three kinds, of which this was the first described by Englemann in 1880 from Ivanpah, then an outpost of the Union Pacific Railroad line in the eastern Mojave Desert. Some workers prefer to treat the three plants as subspecies under *Coryphantha* (or *Mammillaria*) *vivipara*, a widespread species through Arizona, New Mexico, and Sonora, Mexico. The purposes of the present handbook, however, call for the use of different specific names as a matter of convenience.

Coryphantha deserti is a solitary form 3 to 8 inches tall, covered with whitish spines with red-brown tips. The number of radial spines, 20 to 25, is a distinctive character. The flowers are pink, rose, yellowish, or straw-colored (pl. 8, *a*). The flower color seems to differ from area to area.

This species has a more easterly distribution in the Mojave Desert than its near relative, the Foxtail Cactus, and may be observed on rocky hillsides at elevations of 1,500 to 6,000 feet in ranges between Baker and Needles and north into Inyo County. Good colonies may be seen between Cima and Ivanpah and in the Lanfair Valley to the southeast.

Foxtail Cactus (*Coryphantha alversonii*)

A. H. Alverson, prospectors' supplier and desert traveler out of early San Bernardino, discovered this plant on one of his wagon expeditions about 1890 and sent specimens to the United States National Herbarium. It is now recognized as one of the most attractive cacti of the Joshua Tree National Monument. Not only can it be touched with safety, but it produces lovely flowers.

The species is distinguished from its near relative, *Coryphantha deserti*, by its more numerous brown-tipped central spines (12-16) and shorter tubercules. The plants are commonly larger and often have several heads (pl. 8, *c*). The ranges of the two species hardly overlap, for *C. alversonii* is characteristic of the south Mojave Desert, largely within the Joshua Tree National Monument, where the plant is now protected. The Foxtail Cactus does not survive well in cultivation, and in the past thousands of plants were dug up, only to die in coastal gardens. Some of the best remaining colonies may be seen in the Monument around White Tank south of Twentynine Palms, and near Old Dale.

Arizona Pincushion Cactus (*Coryphantha arizonica*)

This is a rare plant in California and in part overlaps the range of *Coryphantha deserti*. It may be distinguished easily, however, by its much larger flowers (pl 8, *d*), and by the smaller number of radial spines (fewer than 20) which allow the tubercles to be seen clearly. The heads are usually solitary and hemispherical, 3 to 4 inches high.

Coryphantha arizonica must be sought in California in easternmost San Bernardino County within 50 to 60 miles of the Nevada boundary, in the New York and Castle Mountains, and between Cima and Goffs in the Lanfair Valley area. It may be found among piñon and juniper in the vicinity of Mitchell's Caverns in the Providence Mountains. During flowering season in May and June the otherwise rather obscure plants are strikingly evident.

Coastal Fishhook Cactus; Nipple Cactus
(*Mammillaria dioica*)

Mammillaria is a large genus of nipple or pincushion cacti sometimes recognized as containing more than 200 species. Most of them are rather small single or clustered plants, and many have hooked spines. Most of the kinds of *Mammillaria* occur in Mexico. Several extend into Arizona, but only two into California. As with *Echinocereus*, some manuals and floras group other related genera such as *Phellosperma* and *Coryphantha* under *Mammillaria*, but for our purposes it seems more effective to recognize the distinctive features of these under different names.

Mammillaria dioica is a plant of San Diego County west of the Borrego Desert. It is often common in the seacoast chaparral and may be observed at the Cabrillo National Monument at Point Loma (pl. 8, e). A somewhat more robust form than the coastal one extends inland through the mountains below 5,000 feet to the western edge of the Colorado Desert. It may be seen in Sentenac Canyon below Julian in the *Opuntia bigelovii* association.

Distinctive characters of *Mammillaria* are often small and should be studied with a hand lens. The outer parts of the flower in *M. dioica*, for example, are not ciliate as in *M. microcarpa*, and there are small bristles in the axils of the tubercles. The stigma lobes are green. The specific name refers to an interesting character in which the flowers are partly dioecious. Some plants, that is, have flowers which are only male or only female.

Desert Fishhook Cactus (*Mammillaria microcarpa*)

This species is characteristically an Arizona plant that occurs within California only in the far western edges of our deserts near the Colorado River. Its only reported range within the state is in the Whipple Mountains near Parker Dam, where much of the char-

acteristic Arizona flora crosses the river, including the
Giant Saguaro.

Mammillaria microcarpa is superficially similar to
both *M. dioica* and *Phellosperma tetrancistra*. It lacks
the corky-based seeds of the latter and the auxiliary
bristles of both. It has only 11 to 30 radial spines. Its
lavender flowers, which usually appear in April, have
distinctive ciliate margins on the perianth segments,
and the stigmas are of a paler color than the green of
M. dioica (fig. 23).

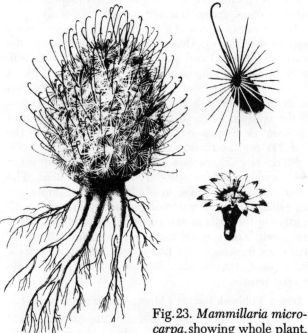

Fig. 23. *Mammillaria microcarpa,* showing whole plant,
spination, and flower.

CACTUS BOOKS AND CLUBS

This is the only book especially on California cacti to have appeared for thirty years. *California Cactus,* by E. M. Baxter, published in 1935, has long been out of print. For those who desire a more comprehensive handbook of the American cacti, the writer's *How to Know the Cacti,* 1963, is available from the Wm. C. Brown Co., Dubuque, Iowa.

Most of the available literature on cacti can be obtained through the Abbey Garden Press, 18007 Topham Street, Reseda, California. The following titles may be of interest to California cactus enthusiasts: *Cacti of San Diego County,* by Lindsay; *Cacti of the Southwest,* by Earle; *Cacti for the Amateur,* by Haselton; *Cactaceae,* by Marshall and Bock; *The Cactaceae* (4 vols.), by Britton and Rose.

The Abbey Garden Press is publication headquarters for the bimonthly *Journal* of the Cactus and Succulent Society of America, which has been published for over thirty years. Persons interested in cacti will enjoy membership in this national society and attendance at its meetings and conventions. There are a number of affiliated cactus societies in California where those of similar interests meet to discuss their plants and pictures. Some of these clubs are in Sacramento, Oakland, San Jose, Bakersfield, Santa Monica, Los Angeles, Hawthorne, Gardena, Long Beach, Victorville, Riverside, Vista, San Diego, and El Centro.

GLOSSARY

arborescent — treelike.

areoles — specialized spots on the body of a cactus bearing hair, wool, glochids, spines, and sometimes leaves; potentially capable of new growth and the production of branches or flowers

axil — the point of divergence of a branch, a leaf, or a tubercle.

central spines — those arising from the center of the areole and more or less erect.

chaparral — a vegetation type of the Southwest characterized by dense, low, coarse brush with few or no trees, capable of rapid regeneration after fires.

ciliate — bearing a fringe of hairlike processes.

deciduous — falling away at maturity.

decumbent — reclining, but with the terminus ascending.

deflexed — bent, curved, or directed downward.

dioecious — plants or flowers in which one flower bears the male, staminate parts, and another bears the female, pistillate parts.

epiphytic — growing on another plant.

glochids — minute spines provided with retuse barbs, characteristic of *Opuntia* and usually found in large numbers in its areoles.

inferior ovary — an ovary situated below the insertion of the perianth segments.

obpyriform — inversely pear-shaped.

ovary — the fleshy basal part of the cactus flower which becomes the fruit.

perianth segments — those parts of the flower corresponding to the petals and sepals when distinction between these is not clear.

porrect — directed outward and forward.

proliferous — reproducing or regenerating freely by offsets.

radial spines — spines arising from the outer part of the areole and oriented radially.

rotate — wheel-shaped when open.

tubercles — protuberances from the fleshy body of the cacti in the form of low or high mounds, or of nipple-like structures.

tuberculate — beset with knobby projections or excrescences.

vascular system — the woody conductive tissue within the fleshy plant body.

[62]

INDEX

Published by

Teresa M. Aquila
Reno, Nevada

www.teresasgarage@gmail.com

TXu-2-083-485

Printed in the United States of America

Pursuit

Both my pants and I had a fresh bullet hole in us, but I'd already decided that I'd be hanged before that cock-eyed para-medic was going to cut my pants.

It was my day off from the Sheriff's Department but not from the school district working swing shift. I was using the morning before beginning my shift at the school district to step back from my life and to find some reasoning for all that was happening.

My job as a heavy duty mechanic for the school district was far from the glory so many newspapers and magazines had portrayed it to be for me. While being a trailblazer and first woman to have ever held this position in the state of Nevada was rewarding, and I was happy to experience the recognition, the pain and suffering proved challenging.

I was trying to distance myself even for one day from all my daily turmoil and to shift myself from defensive to offensive. It was hard to do. I made a promise to take this morning off and not think about feeling sorry for myself, but, instead, be productive and reassure myself as to why I had chosen to be a mechanic.

The morning was calm, and I was deep into putting my house in order, cleaning and performing house chores per my weekly routine. Listening to my favorite 60s music and freeing my thoughts of anything that even resembled negativity, I was in pretty good spirits. At 8:30 a.m., the phone rang. I picked up the receiver,

6

"Hello, Teresa?"

"Yes, who's calling?"

"This is Sgt. Melton,"

"Hey Sgt., what's up?"

"I hate to ask this, but are you able to come in now and work a dayshift? We are short staffed and could really use your help."

"To be honest, Sergeant, I have lunch plans with a friend before I had to work at the school district," I answered.

"I hate to ask, but we really need you today," he replied.

I was never one to say no when it came to requests from the Sheriff's Department. I thought about this request for a moment, then replied, "OK, if you really need me, I can come in, but I need to be out of there by 1:30 so I can be at work by 2 pm."

"OK, great. I promise you'll be out by 2 pm. Thank you so much Teresa. I'll see you when you get here." I hung up the phone.

Unfortunately, I wasn't able to get hold of my friend to cancel our lunch date, but I knew she would understand (this was long before the existence of cell phones). Life happened, and instant communication was unavailable at the time.

I grabbed my duty gear and headed to the brand new station that had opened only a month earlier. It was closer to my house and state-of-the-art – a complete change from the old facility which still housed metal bars on the jail door like the ones you see in old western movies.

When I arrived I headed up to the second floor where the patrol division was located, and I made my way to the sergeant's office to check in with Sgt. Melton.

"Hey, Sergeant, I made it. What beat do you want me to handle today?" I asked.

"Good morning, Teresa. Thank you for helping us out today. We only have three other patrol units on duty today. I need you to take Beat 17. I have a car for you; it's checked out already. Here are the keys. Again, thank you so much for coming in on such short notice. You have made my day."

Little did I know what a day it would become.

I headed to the women's locker room and changed into my uniform, giving my appearance a once over, making sure all my gear was in place, and that I was ready for the unexpected. I felt relieved that the Sgt. had pre-assigned my patrol car. (All too often finding an available unit was an adventure.)

I circled the patrol car, giving it a once-over, checking the lights and tires, and inspecting for any previous damage. I opened the trunk and loaded my equipment. Everything looked perfect. Getting into the driver's seat and thankful for electric controls, I adjusted the seat and mirrors before signing on with Dispatch.

"Dispatch, 1721," I spoke into my radio.

"1721, go ahead," dispatch replied. I recognized the voice, it was my friend Sharon.

"I'm 10-41 (beginning duty) and 10-8 (ready for assignment)."

"Good morning, 10-63, (prepare to copy assignment)."

"10-67 (prepare to copy)."

"Respond to 10285 Bybee Lane on destruction of property that occurred last evening. The homeowner has called several times and is waiting for your arrival."

"10-4," I affirmed.

The call location was close to the station, so my travel time was only 10 minutes. I was thinking that, since the incident had occurred the previous evening, the homeowner was probably going to be angry. So I contemplated my strategy, hoping to mollify the complainant irritation due to our slow response time.

Upon arriving, I was met by the homeowner, an average-appearing woman in her 50s – her body language exhibiting, loud and clear, her annoyance at our tardiness. Working my gift of gab to calm her down, I scanned her property to generate some mutual interest. Noting that she had horses out back (and being a horse owner myself), I sparked a conversation about her love of horses, which helped to create a rapport between us.

"We are very sorry for taking so long to respond, but I am here now. What can I help you with, Leslie?"

"Late last night someone threw a rock or something into my sliding glass door. It scared me to death and broke the glass. Let me show you,"

She pointed to a side of the residence, escorting me where the broken sliding door was located. I began to ask a few questions,

"About what time did this occur?"

"Sometime around 10:00 pm."

"Did you see anyone or hear a vehicle?"

"No. It was late, and I was heading to bed, when suddenly I heard this loud noise and glass shattering. That is when I called the sheriff's office. My son actually went outside to see if he could see or hear anyone, but he couldn't."

"OK, Leslie, let me get to work and see what I can come up with."

I quickly began investigating the crime, glancing at the sliding glass door from inside and checking to make sure the second pane was still intact. Once outside, I examined the broken glass to determine what type of projectile had been used to cause the destruction. After my initial scan of the crime scene, I went to the car to retrieve the documents required to complete the report, grabbing my clipboard and securing the report form.

I made it as far as placing Leslie's name on the case report when I began to hear the emergency tones blaring from my radio on my duty belt. Beep, Beep, Beep. I froze, listening to my radio. It was Dispatch reporting that a unit was involved in a pursuit and that they were heading my direction from the south.

I gave my radio a solid grip and chimed in. "Dispatch, 1721."

"1721, go ahead," dispatch responded.

"I am in the area of the pursuit; do you wish me to respond?"

"Yes, if you can. Other units are too far out."

I turned to the homeowner, knowing she was not going to be happy for what I was about to say after she had waited all night for a deputy to show up.

"Leslie, I hate to tell you this, but I have to go and help with an emergency. I will be back!"

I jumped into my patrol car, my adrenalin intensifying as I sped down the road in the direction of the pursuit heading my way.

"Dispatch, can you advise on the pursuit location?"

A whirlwind of information was coming over the radio as the pursuing unit constantly updated his location. The dispatcher's transmission was cutting in and out due to the high level of activity, but I thought I

11

had deciphered most of it, and it seemed that she had indicated the unit had already passed my location.

Wow, they must be flying, I thought.

When I arrived at the intersection that would put me on the same road as the pursuit, I made a right turn, assuming they had already gone by. There did not appear to be any activity ahead of me. I glanced up into my rearview and saw in the distance the patrol unit's overhead lights. Obviously, they had not in fact passed me.

I pulled over for a moment, waiting for them to catch up to me when I thought, *Wait what if they stop further back and I am here waiting while they need assistance in apprehending the suspect?*

I decided to make a u-turn and advance to the officers' location. I knew that if they managed to pass me I could quickly turn around and join in on the pursuit. My radar gun was going crazy; the numbers were unbelievable. The suspect was traveling beyond 120 mph with patrol unit 1711 hot on his tail.

When the suspect saw me coming towards him, he moved into my lane, heading straight for me. I glanced at my speedometer. I was traveling 40 mph. I tried moving slightly to one side to clear his path, No good – he moved with me.

OK. Now I knew I was going to have to play chicken with the suspect, and I hoped it would work. Everything seemed to go in slow motion, my senses heightened as the car kept speeding straight at me

One side of my brain was screaming for me to get out of the way while the other side stayed calm and focused, guiding me through the moment. *Hold it, hold it Teresa. Not yet. Hold it.* Closer and closer we raced towards each other until we were seconds away from a collision.

NOW!

Simultaneously, we both swerved off to our respective right sides, barely missing each other. We were both able to keep control of our vehicles. *Dammit, I thought. I was hoping he would over-correct and lose control.* No such luck. Now the suspect's vehicle was passing me on my left and I was able to get a good look at his face. The smile of a maniac sneered at me as if to say *you are about to die.*

It was then that I heard a loud BOOM!

Before my brain could register what was happening, I thought *damn what a horrible time to have a blowout.* Somehow, however, I knew that that wasn't quite right, as I moved my head side to side for some reason that was not yet clear to me. It was only a split second before I realized that something had hit my left leg (my braking leg), causing me to slam on the brakes.

The pursuing unit kept close on the suspect's tail, not letting up. I took a deep breath and began looking around for what had hit me. I turned to my left noticing that the door panel to my patrol car was blown apart. It was definitely not a tire I blew out. I had been shot. Blood was everywhere.

It is amazing what your body is capable of in moments like that and even crazier how your emotions work. My adrenaline was in overdrive; I was determined to keep going. I knew that there were only four of us on duty that day and that manpower was short, so I had to keep going. I was their wing man, and I could not let them down.

I radioed to dispatch, "1721 has been shot, I repeat, I have been shot." My voice was surprisingly calm.

"I am continuing in the pursuit," I stated.

Sharon had immediately dispatched an ambulance my direction, when she heard me say I was shot. She did not; however hear me when I stated I was continuing in the pursuit.

I floor-boarded it to catch up, exceeding 120mph myself. All that kept going through my head was that famous line by the Wicked Witch of the West in the *Wizard of Oz,* "I'll get you my pretty" on repeat over and over again. I could hear her nasally voice. "I'll get you my pretty...I'll get you my pretty."

Dispatch was on overload, but Sharon was a pro who kept me calm, while trying to persuaded me to pull over. When the medics realized I was still in pursuit they began chasing me while I chased the suspect. It was an unorthodox situation, to say the least.

This went on for about eight miles until I could tell my body was starting to go into shock, and the pain in my knee was quickly building. I knew I had to pull over

14

and seek medical attention. At least the medics weren't that far behind me.

I took the nearest off ramp that the suspect traveled and pulled over onto the right shoulder of the road. I got out of my car to inspect my injury and examine the bullet hole in my car door. I was bleeding profusely, but I had been lucky. The bullet had travelled through both the suspect's car door and mine, slowing it down and its potential impact before it hit the back of my knee, inflicting a deep, canal-like wound across the entire width of my leg.

The medics arrived with their sirens blaring and lights flashing. The passenger medic was out of the vehicle before it even came to a full stop, rushing to my aid. He inspected my wound, identifying it as serious, before proceeding to pull out a pair of scissors from his bag, kneeling down behind me to cut away my pant leg.

"You're not going to cut my pants, are you?" I objected

"Yes I am, Deputy. I need to access your wound. I can't treat it without cutting your pant leg off," he stated.

"What? Oh, no, you're not!" I exclaimed, turning toward him. He looked at me, dumbfounded.

My strong protest was due to a change which the Sheriff's Office was undertaking by removing the classic black strip along the side of our pant legs. For me, the strip appeared professional, and I was not a fan of the new design. However, the Command Staff had offered all deputies the option of wearing the original style pants if they already owned them. Allowing the medic to cut off my pant leg meant I would have to bow down to the new style.

Yes, I was more concerned about my pants than my wound. Forget about being shot, my damaged knee, or bleeding out on the side of road. Oh no, it was all about my pants. Funny the way our minds can work in high-stress situations. In any case, the medic, realizing I was serious but also in a considerably agitated, attempted to reason with me.

"Well Deputy, if you won't let me cut your pants, then you will need to drop your drawer's right here, right now, so I can address your wound."

He looked up at me, waiting a beat or two for me to decide.

It was in that moment that I halted. I suddenly had become aware of my surroundings and the situation I was in. I saw that a small crowd had already begun to gather at all of the commotion, and there was no way I was going to drop my pants and expose everything to the world. I closed my eyes, and, with a sigh of resignation, relented.

"Go for it, before I change my mind".

He wasted no time before I heard the snip, snip, snip, of the scissors circling around my leg before the medic – how dare he! – threw the amputated fabric to the ground. This travesty hurt me more than my wound.

Expressing concern about my current state, he summoned me to the ambulance for medical attention.

Stubborn as ever, I, of course, had to stop first to pick up the cut material from my pants.

"Maybe they can still be mended?" I suggested.

I hobbled to the back of the ambulance, not wanting to bend my left knee or add too much pressure to the wound, and watched as the medic pulled the gurney onto the street, positioning it in front of me. Failing to recognize that he had yet to lock it into the proper upright position, I hopped onto it prematurely.

Bizarre police chase, shooting

Driver kills himself after allegedly firing gun at deputy

Wounded officer continued pursuit

That was a mistake. Once my body made contact with the unsecured gurney, which collapsed with me on top of it, causing me to be thrown off and forcing my left leg to bend. A streak of hot pain seared through my body; I saw only black spots for a few moments. Damn, that hurt!

I am sure that at this point the medics were tired of me and not at all amused with my performance. Here they were, trying to render aid to me, and I was causing one hindrance after another. The medic who had been

17

first at my side huffed as he helped me onto the gurney, now fully secured. I could tell by the look on his face I was a pain in his backside.

By now the local newspapers had arrived, and, as the medic helped me on to the gurney, I could hear the click, click, clicking of the cameras. Photographers and reporters were capturing my wounded and miserable condition. *At least I am having a great hair day*, I thought.

Even amid everything happening to me – my pain, my emotions, my fevered thoughts – I could still hear and understand the medic conversing with a trauma doctor at the public hospital. *Public hospital*? My brain registered and I grabbed the medic's hand,

"Look. I am Catholic; we are going to St. Mary's hospital."

"But, Deputy, they are not the trauma center the public hospital is."

"Too bad," I asserted, placing my right hand on my duty belt. "If I have to hijack this bus myself, I will. We are going to St. Mary's," I stated with determination and humor but without threat or anger.

I guess he did not think I was very funny, because he called my patrol supervisor to the scene. When the supervisor arrived, he rushed to my side to check on my condition. Honestly, I didn't know he was on the scene, or when and how he got there, but things were happening around me in both a fast forward and slow motion. It all felt so surreal.

"Teresa, why are you threatening the medics who are trying to treat you?"

"It wasn't really a threat, but, I am serious about being taken to the hospital of my choice."

The medic then radioed the Public hospital, indicating we were changing our plan and heading to St. Mary's hospital. After we were underway, I kept rising; looking out the back window, checking to make sure the scenery was in sync with the desired route. I have no doubt at that point the medic wanted nothing more than to sedate – or strangle – me.

Once we had arrived at the hospital, the medics rushed me into Emergency. While waiting to be prepped for surgery, suddenly I remembered I had to work at the school district that afternoon.

I called out to my supervisor. "Please call my other employer at the School District. Let them know I am going to be a little late for work."

"Late?" He chuckled, "You mean out for at least a week or two?"

"Oh, no. Only for a day or two."

I wasn't taking the situation lightly by any means; but, with everyone around me concerned and worried, I was trying to let them know I was OK.

"OK, Teresa, I'm on it," he said, walking off to make the call.

When the supervisor returned, he assured me that my School District boss knew I wouldn't be arriving for work that day,

"I also have an update on the pursuit,"

"What happened? Is everyone else OK?"

"Yes," he replied, to my relief.

He further reported that multiple law enforcement agencies from all over the area were hot on the tail of the suspect, who was returning to where the pursuit started, traveling through residential areas, when he began to slow down. The highway patrolman behind him saw him pull out his revolver, no doubt the same one he shot me with, and shoot himself in the head.

He continued to explain that after the suspect shot himself, his car slowed, veering to the right into a field before coming to rest. The responding officers approached the vehicle with caution and confirmed the suspect was deceased.

It is hard to express how I felt. I didn't have time to really process everything, and I still had my wound to deal with. The bullet had entered through the back or crook of my knee and exited out the other side, creating a deep gash of about a half or 3/4 of an inch thick. It had essentially created a big crater in the back of my knee. On top of that, debris from the car door had also entered the wound and other areas of my leg, embedded deep into my skin. Surgery was scheduled.

Working hard to stay in control, I remained conscious during the surgery, my leg completely numb.

In the room was another Deputy as part of the investigation, maintaining a chain of custody for the fragments embedded in my leg and knee.

I looked on as the surgeon dove in, cutting the skin with his surgical blade, placing pins near the areas where the debris was lodged inside. I was still wearing my now-deformed uniform pants, determined not to relinquish them to the hospital. I maintained silence as scissors appeared in the doctor's hands in order for him to remove a sliver of remaining material from the wound.

Lying on the gurney, slightly elevated, at my altitude I could see that the wound was deep. Focusing laser-like on the surgery, I came to my senses for a brief moment and realized that the operating room housed others not involved with the surgery.

As the doctor prepared to enter the wound, I thought about how embarrassing it might be if I had the inclination to cry. My attention immediately shifted back to the doctor as I observed him digging out pieces of the car. I didn't dare flinch; the opening was big enough.

The wound being open and deep, the doctor couldn't just sew it up. It had to heal from the inside out. That meant a scab would need to form on its own. Medication was applied to the wound to keep infection from forming and before it was bandaged.

The hospital staff asked whether I wished to remain overnight for observation or released home. I opted to go home. I wanted my own bed and familiar surroundings. I was transported home by the Sheriff's Office Chaplain to recover.

At this point I was flying high from both the pain medication and my adrenaline still working overtime. Because I was living alone at the time, I didn't have anyone to care for me or serve as a much-needed voice of reason. So when my phone started ringing off the hook the moment I returned home, there was no one there to answer it or screen the callers for me. As it turned out, every newspaper and news station in town was calling for an interview.

Luckily, I had sense enough not to take the calls; however, I soon needed to distance myself from the constant ringing. Noticing my neighbor in front of his garage, sitting in his favorite chair in the driveway, I decided to join him. He instantly noticed my bandaged leg.

"Teresa, you look like you have been in a bad accident. What happened?" he asked.

"Not an accident, a shooting. I was shot today during a pursuit of a suspect," I said rather nonchalantly. I was still in shock.

My neighbor looked at me as though I had grown another head, "Wow! OK. And you want to sit here and talk with me?"

"Yes, my phone is ringing off the wall, and, with all the drugs pumped into me, during surgery I think it is best not to answer the phone."

"Oh, I see," he said. "So what happened? How did it end?"

"The suspect decided to commit suicide during the pursuit after he shot me." Not a moment after those words left my mouth, I realized how crazy this little visit was. I couldn't believe I was sitting there upright with him and not in bed, where clearly I should have been. Feeling woozy, I retreated back home, and lay down on the couch.

The phone rang relentlessly, it never stopped ringing. Whenever my answering machine picked up, the caller would hang up and then call back right away. I should have unplugged the phone from the wall, but my brain was not working at its full capacity. Instead, seeking some reprieve from the sound, I finally caved and answered the phone. It was the media wanting interviews.

"Hello?"

"Is this Teresa Aquila?"

"Yes. What can I do for you?" I asked, slightly slurring my words.

"This is Channel 4, and we would like to do a live interview about the shooting this morning".

"I will need to check with my supervisor."

"OK. Let me call your station and see if we can obtain approval.'

I hung up the phone, barely removing my hand from it when it rang again. This time it was Channel 8, also inquiring for an interview. Then Channel 2. In my entire career I had never been in a situation such as this, and I was unsure about what to do. I realized I needed to contact my supervisor directly. To my surprise, he approved the interviews.

I should have been in bed recovering, but NO – not me. At this point, most of the news stations had arrived at my home for an in-person interview. One news channel went so far as escorting me to their station. Of course, the drugs were doing their job and my face expressed it. I was interviewed with glassy eyes, a tired appearance, and slow speech. I should have been in bed. What was I thinking? Oh wait; on pain medication, I wasn't thinking.

My recovery was going to be a long one due to the depth of the wound. Still, after only five days of rest, I decided to return to work at the School District. It wasn't a smart move, however; with all of the flak I had already received there, I didn't want to give them any more ammunition.

In fact, all the media attention only created more distance and dislike towards me from my male co-workers. They clearly felt that the shooting was an attention-seeking device. *Attention? Are they kidding? What? So I paid this criminal to shoot me so I could be the center of attention? That was their logic?* This lunacy blew my mind, and it still does.

In light of my insistence on returning to work, my boss gave me a light duty job, which was to refresh the lettering on the school buses.

The downfall to performing this job was it required me to elevate myself. I knew there was a tall chair in the shop, which I sought out to help alleviate pressure from my knee. Somehow said chair ended up missing in action, and no one seemed to know where it went or offered any assistance in finding it. I ended up having to perform the assignment standing up.

I made it through the shift but at the expense of traumatizing my knee. Once I arrived home from work that evening, my leg blew up like a balloon, swollen and painful. I knew icing it would help, but I was worried. I called the ER and received a prescription for pain killers – on which I declined to follow up because I had never been one to take opiates, which always made me feel sick. So I suffered through the pain.

The next day, my knee wasn't faring any better, so I once again contacted the ER. I was explicitly forbidden to return to work. I was quickly scheduled to have an orthopedist examine the wound. Now, I was feeling rather foolish for trying to prove to my co-workers that not even a bullet could keep me down. I had thought those sexist men would think I was a baby, and I wanted to prove otherwise to them. My decision-making had been clouded by their behavior, and I had let them into my head. My common sense hadn't been functioning, and my choices proved that.

My focus should have been on my healing. I had just gone through a life-threatening ordeal, both physically and mentally; but I was more concerned about my job at the School District. I knew at this point that the shooting was only going to add another reason for co-workers to dislike me. As if the media attention I had received previously was not irritating enough, this latest episode would only intensify their hostility towards me. However, in order for my leg to heal, it was imperative that I stay off it. This was one of those damned-if-you-do-damned-if-you-don't situations. In any case, a note directed to my employer stated that I would not be released to return to work for a minimum of 6 weeks – if not longer.

On schedule, I arrived for my first appointment with the orthopedist, Dr. Johnson, one week after the shooting. Our first encounter was far from pleasurable. Dr. Johnson removed my bandage, and this was the first time I really viewed my injury.

It was not pretty; there was a hole deep across the crook of my left knee. Dr. Johnson took one look at it and said, "Teresa, this is going to be painful. You aren't carrying your gun today are you?" Thank goodness he had a great sense of humor.

"No. Should I be?"

Now I was worried. What was I in for? The doctor asked me to lay face-down on the table, placing my leg straight out. Not taking my eyes off of him (partly out of curiosity, but mostly out of fear), I wanted to see firsthand what instrument of torture he was going to use on me.

It was then that he pushed a piece of wood in my face, similar to a tongue depressor, and told me to bite down on it.

"Bite down?" I asked.

"Yes. I need to remove the scab from the entire wound, and it will be painful."

My face contorting with anguish, my lips clenched tight together to comfort me as my teeth ground back and forth. I felt my breathing quickened in anticipation of the pain that was about to arrive. My body began to quiver as I did what the doctor asked, biting down on the chunk of wood, not knowing how painful this scab ripping procedure was going to be. I took a deep breath.

Then it happened, I felt him grab tight on one end of the scab and RIP, he yanked it off. My teeth dug into that piece of wood so hard I thought they were going to crack. I exhaled in hopes of releasing the pain I was feeling. My heart was pounding, tears filling my eyes, my body trembling the intensity of the pain. My wound was now bleeding, and I thought, *hell no, I am not coming back for any more of this*! This hurt worse than actually getting shot.

Lying on the table, attempting to regain my composure amid a torrent of tears, I worked hard in the attempt to extinguish the burning sensation from my wound. Dr. Johnson worked quickly to reduce the bleeding, applying disinfectant and antibiotics.

As I reeled with the ripping pain, the doctor applied gauze to the injured area, then wrapped it with white medical tape.

"This is a serious wound. I will need to see you weekly for at least six weeks to repeat the cleaning process. It is the only way to allow a wound this deep to heal from the inside out."

My eyes enlarged as hot fear rocketed through me. "You mean I have to experience this wonderful scab ripping six more times? And I am supposed to be excited about that?"

"Well, I can't promise to excite you, but I do have a large supply of wood for your pleasure."

"Pleasure . . . I'd rather get shot again than come here and experience this again."

It was going to be a long six weeks and a painful road to recovery.

INSPIRATION OF A LIFETIME

The seriousness of my wound left me idle by doctor's orders to remain off the leg and off work for at least six weeks. The thought of sitting around the house watching TV or listening to the radio spelled boredom in my mind.

Lying in bed one morning moderately on pain medication, with my wounded knee propped up on a pillow, reminiscing my past, gave me the opportunity to reflect on how I ended up in this basket – how the passion I developed early on for law and order and everything mechanical developed.

Many go through life wondering what profession is the right one to pursue or even what they want out of life. In my case, I had my sights focused on two (at the time) unconventional careers, not realizing that women held a certain place in society. I envisioned my adult life to be filled with enforcing the law and working as a female gear-head turning wrenches.

I arrived in this world on September 21, 1954, when poodle skirts and black leather jackets were all the rage and before the Beatles – when going to diners and sharing milkshakes were typical first dates while tunes like "Earth Angel" and "Susie Q" played from every jukebox. It was before President Kennedy was shot and The Vietnam War consumed our everyday life.

I was born into an Italian-American family as the third child of five. Both of my parents were born to Italian immigrants and the culture was always a big part of our lives. My mother, Jean, was a soft-spoken person, appearing tall to me, with a confidence that exuded from her every expression. My mother and I never really had a close relationship; it was my sister, Ana, who seemed to have that close relationship with her.

Ana was five years older than I and the first child. She was a dainty soul, prim and proper; I guess you could say she was a girl's girl. Next in line was my brother Jay, who I was closest to. I, a tomboy in every respect, followed by my two younger brothers, Gary and Don. It must have been the tomboy in me that drove me closer to my father than my mother. I was never dainty; from the get-go, I liked things the boys liked: helping my dad polish the car, working with tools, making kites and hanging out with my father. I have to admit, my mother sure gave it her best shot to feminize me – not without my resistance.

My father was not a tall man, but in my eyes he was a giant and my hero: Italian descent, short hair, and a smile that could captivate you when he entered the room. He was a butcher, a meat cutter in today's terms, and he owned his own meat market. He ran the family business as part of the Farmer's Market in Richmond, California, east of San Francisco. My dad was both a hardworking husband and dedicated father. He was meticulous in everything he did, most often busy with work; still, he was very influential to me in my beginning years.

My father was always extremely patient with me. For example, during my first couple of weeks in kindergarten, he sat in the car in front of my classroom in order to comfort me with his presence.

Meeting my teacher, Miss Moon, had been more of an overwhelming experience than a harmonious one for me. Not only was it my first day of school, it was my first encounter meeting a black person. I will never forget that moment, not even today. She was a large woman, wearing bright red lipstick whose dark hair lay loosely on her head; she wore a black dress that fit her well and went down just past her knees. I really gave her the once-over and quickly grabbed my mother's leg, screaming. I was horrified to think that my parents would leave me here with this strange woman. Of course, at the time I had no knowledge of any issues between blacks or whites; it was her red lipstick that set me off.

I was set on going back home with my mom and not being left behind; it seemed my mother knew that was not an option for me but had failed to let me in on the decision. I swear she dragged me into the classroom before sashaying off. Needless to say, I spent the rest of this first day looking out the window just waiting to see my mom's car pull up to take me away from this horrible experience.

I actually did survive the first day and was firm on not returning to relive this experience. One day was more than enough for this little girl. Well, at least that is what I thought. I was brought back the next day to face it all over again, only this time, my dad parked his Chevy coupe out front so I could see that he was there just in case I needed to yell for help or run like hell.

This went on for a few days until I became more accustomed to my new adventure in life: kindergarten and Miss Moon. It did not take long for us to become comfortable with each other. Now looking back, that had to be a milestone for Miss Moon as well, being a black female teacher in an all-white school in 1959.

She really was someone special, because she never made students feel as if any one of us was lesser than the other, only treating everyone with kindness and respect. In return, we did the same for her.

Nevertheless, that first year of school was rather hard on me, and I'm sure my parents didn't feel it was any picnic either. I became very sick with everything you could imagine; the mumps, measles, chicken pocks, and tonsillitis (numerous times), which forced the school to keep me back another year due to my absences.

It was a sad moment when I discovered that I would not be advancing to first grade alongside my classmates; it seemed my kindergarten seat would be waiting for me the next school year. I was devastated with the ordeal. The other classmates – who once were on the same level as I – now made fun of me because I had to be held back. It was disappointing and heart wrenching for this six-year-old.

As I grew older, I really began to enjoy and cherish school. So many people in this world do not have the opportunity to learn and better themselves. Learning is a privilege and it has helped mold the person I am today. School became something I detested missing, even when I was sick and should have been in bed. If I was unable to attend school, I knew I was missing out on something great. It is through school that I experienced a special encounter that changed my life forever. I will never forget that spring day. I was in first grade and about to discover my calling in life.

I was attending Mira Vista Elementary School, in Richmond, California, during a time when our country was between wars, but enlistment for young men was in full swing. We were growing as a nation. I had not yet been exposed to segregation between blacks and whites, or the horrors of what the Vietnam War would bring, so life was still sweet.

This was a time when the Principal's razor strap ruled the school hanging from his door as a reminder of what was to happen in case you felt the need to get out of line. Every time I passed by it, I walked slowly and as far from it as possible. Getting the strap was not on my agenda, so staying on the good side of my teachers was a top priority. (Others, though, had to learn the hard way.)

Now, those who were not so juvenile were given the bike yard. What was the bike yard? Well, there was an area outside of the classrooms, heading into the playground, where kids could park their bikes and where white lines were painted. If you had the displeasure of being sent there as punishment, you would have to stand on one of the white lines during recess so the entire world could see you messed up. I have to confess, I had to visit that famous line of detention at least once during my six years there.

During my first-grade school year, my teacher, Miss Collins, was always so gracious to have featured guests visit our classroom and teach us new and exciting things. But little did I know that one visitor would present a life-changing experience.

One sunny spring day, we were told that a special visitor was coming to talk to us about safety. As we stood and welcomed our special guest from the Richmond Police Department, he entered, dressed in blue with the coolest belt of things hanging from his hips that not only sparkled in the sunlight but piqued my curiosity. I wanted to learn what everything was used for. Towering above us, his face broke into a warm smile.

"Hello, everyone. My name is Officer Little. Please take your seats". I was mesmerized from that moment on. I couldn't take my eyes off of him. It was like this bolt of lightning had hit me. I absorbed every word he spoke, and I knew right then that I wanted to be a police officer.

Officer Little discussed topics ranging from staying safe from kidnapping, to not playing in the street, to awareness of your surroundings, to always obeying the law. What I took from that message was that if you did break the law, it wouldn't be the strap or the lonely bike yard; it would be what I called the Big House. Officer Little was more compassionate about the consequences; he referred to it as a Juvenile Detention. You could hear my classmates gasp at the thought of it. *No thanks,* I thought.

Officer Little allowed us the privilege of learning about all the tools he carried on his duty belt. I recall that he carried only a nightstick, flashlight, revolver, and handcuffs – half of what an officer needs in today's world.

Once Officer Little had completed his classroom discussion, we were all asked to follow him outside for a huge treat. I stuck close to him, because following in his footsteps was where I wanted to be – not to mention (or have I already mentioned?) I loved looking at all the tools on his belt. Even the sounds they made with his every step fascinated me.

As we all walked down the hallway, past the Principal's dreaded belt, we exited outside, where we gazed our first glance of his bright shiny police car. I could not believe my eyes; it was a 1959 Ford Custom 4 door, black and white with red lights on the top – the same treatment as Mayberry RFD's car on the Andy Griffith Show.

After the initial *oohs* and *ahhs,* Officer Little, turned to us and seriously intoned, "Now who wants to see the inside first?"

I was excited as a bag of jumping beans. Adding to the excitement, he gave each of us the opportunity to sit behind the steering wheel, turn on the red lights and play the siren. After what felt like forever, my turn came, and, once inside the car, I did not want to leave. As if his duty belt hadn't been impressive enough, this experience definitely set in stone my calling from that moment on. I knew that being a police officer would be in my future.

At the end of his visit, Officer Little told all of us that if we ever saw him on the streets, to stick out our first and last fingers, while curling the others, and wiggle them at him. That way he would remember that we had met him before – which for me would be a secret signal between me and the man who was now my major inspiration.

The Aftermath

Two weeks after the shooting, still reeling from some negative publicity, I was skeptical about venturing out of the house. I hadn't heard from anyone at the Sheriff's Office and was curious as to the whereabouts of my briefcase that had been in my patrol car that day.

A girlfriend of mine, Judy Johnson, offered to take me to the office to check in and grab my briefcase. Besides all the media interviews occurring right after the incident, I had not traveled outside the house except to the doctor's office. I was reluctant to venture out. I wasn't sure what to expect, nor was I sure if I was ready for questions from strangers recognizing me from all the media attention.

Arriving at the station, I was greeted by fellow employees who inquired about my well-being. Patrol was on the second floor; Judy and I took the elevator, because trying to master 20 stairs was not a task I was ready to accomplish. Once in Patrol, I found my briefcase sitting in the briefing room in a corner.

My former partner, Sergeant Markel, walked by at that moment and noticed me in the room. He appeared shocked to see me.

"Teresa, what are you doing here?"

"Well, Sergeant, I wanted to make sure my briefcase still existed, and here it is," I answered, holding the item up for him to see.

Encountering Sergeant Markel led me into reflecting on my earlier years as a Deputy, when he had been a fine partner to me. He always offered me great praise when warranted and harsh criticism when needed. Always looking out for my best interest, he was determined to make me a good cop.

I will never forget the night we were working a shift together, responding to a call involving a rollover accident. As he drove us to the scene, he turned to me.

"Teresa, I want you to know that I do not allow just anyone to be my partner. But *you* – you can work at my side anytime."

Coming from Sergeant Markel, then a Deputy, this was a huge compliment. It was at that moment that I knew I was now a part of the team.

Ending my reverie and snapping back into the present, I wished Sergeant Markel a good day and proceeded to check my office mailbox which I was sure must have been overflowing at this point. It was crammed full, as suspected, and I tucked the mail under my arm. I would sort through it all when I got home.

I was almost out the front door when I was approached by Lt. Patterson, the jail supervisor.

"Hi, Teresa, how are you doing?"

"Fine, Sir. Thanks for asking."

"I just wanted to check on you. This has been such a traumatic incident that I wanted to make sure you are doing well both physically and mentally."

"Lt. Patterson, I really appreciate your concerns, but I really am doing well – just need time to heal and get back to all my jobs."

"If you need anything, please let me know. Has anyone here contacted you about the shooting?"

"No, Sir. Not yet."

"I have a meeting with the Sheriff; I will mention it to him. You take care and call if you need anything."

"Thank you, Sir, I will."

As I turned to leave, another employee, Candy Thomas, came running up to me.

"Teresa, I'm glad to see you are doing better. Have you seen today's paper?"

"No. I haven't been looking at the paper in fear of negative press, and I need downtime right now. And the stories could be hard to swallow if they're negative."

"Well, you should read this one; it's a letter to the editor from a lady who lives in Carson City."

I should have stuck to my original plan, keeping my distance from any media. The letter in question had been printed in the local newspaper, which was a major medium at the time.

Grabbing the paper, I began to read this letter, dated May 24, 1988:

Putting the paper down, I felt my emotions hit rock bottom. Where did this lady get the idea that I wasn't shot – which I definitely was? I had no intentions of taking this suspect's life; I only wanted to free the streets of a dangerous individual. I was deeply depressed by the thought that someone would feel so negative about me and assume that I was a horrible person for protecting lives. I was trembling, close to tears. Having been flying high on adrenaline for days, I was slammed to the ground by this letter.

Turning to Judy, I said, "Please, let's go home; I need to get out of here."

Leaving the newspaper behind, I quickly left the building. Judy kept asking me if I was OK.

All I could say was, "I'm fine. But how can a person without knowing all the facts be so hurtful – so unfair?"

39

This latest aggravation made me want to lock myself inside my house and avoid the phone or visitors. While the shooting had not depressed me, this letter to the newspaper definitely did the trick.

After settling in at home, I took a deep breath trying to exhale the anxiety arriving from my first venture out since the shooting. I began sorting through my Sheriff's Office mail, hoping to find some distraction.

The mail was the usual stuff I normally received: reports that needing extra attention and more detail, a few get-well messages, and announcements of upcoming events. I noticed nothing significant until I picked up an envelope, appearing to contain a card, addressed in a youthful handwriting. Reluctant to open it, in fear of a negative message, I inhaled and ripped along the top of it.

Glancing at the front of it, I could see that it was a get well card, the front portraying a superhero-type character. As I opened the card, tears began pooling in my eyes as I read its message:

Dear Deputy Aquila, thank you for protecting us, and I'm glad you're OK. You are my hero. Sincerely, David Cotter.

Frozen at the moment, emotions building within me, I felt a single tear roll down my right cheek.

I was in awe to know that a 12-year-old boy, David Cotter, from Mamie Towles Elementary School, had sent me, a complete stranger, a get-well card and called me his hero. I must have reread the card a hundred times, each time releasing new tears. The timing for such a heartwarming gift could not have been more propitious.

This one selfless, beautiful gesture helped me step out of my depression and realize that I was in fact making a difference by putting my life on the line. My self-assurance began to rebuild, validating my commitment to protect and to serve. The feeling of confidence rushed through me as if it had never deserted me. I had needed some reassurance that my law enforcement career hadn't been for nothing. This special card provided that to me.

Prior to my return to work, it became my mission to connect with this amazing young man. I contacted the school that David attended. Luckily, the school was able to reach out to him on my behalf.

I wanted to do something special for this extraordinary young man and give him a little part of myself, similar to the gift that he had given me during my time of need. I wanted him to know of the profound benefit his card had brought to my morale – and that his thoughtfulness had struck me as the miracle of a young heart reaching out with a blessed expression of gratitude to someone who sorely needed to hear such words.

Filled with excitement, I reached out to the Sheriff's Office Chaplain, I presented my idea to him. I wanted to present David with a plaque engraved with my badge and kind words to express appreciation after not only from me but all those in law enforcement who place their lives daily to protect the citizenry. The Chaplain and I collaborated on the message for several days until it was perfect.

I wanted the presentation to be special. I wanted David's friends to see how a small gesture can change a life. Contemplating the best approach, I chose to present the plaque to David at his school in the presents of his classmates. I wanted them all to know that he was my hero – just as I was his.

The local media heard of this presentation and requested to be present, but I declined to have them attend. This was a moment not for media or the public but between us. Not to be sensationalized, this was to be a personal acknowledgement.

Arriving at the school, maintaining a low profile, I was nervous and excited about meeting David. I did not know what to expect. Walking into his classroom, I inhaled as the sound of cheers filled the room. As the teacher introduced me to her class, a sense of pride swept over me. David rose, smiling broadly, and stepped proudly toward me.

At that point I announced, "Thank you for allowing me this opportunity to be here today. I am here to present a plaque to one of your classmates for offering his kind heart to me, on a day that I needed it most."

Presenting the plaque to David, I turned to face him.

"David, this is to show my extreme appreciation for your kind gesture during a difficult time and for opening my eyes to how events have an impact on young lives. To you, David, I offer this plaque."

An image of the plaque presented to David Cotter

This was the beginning of a special friendship. David and I have spent time together as friends whenever time has allowed. He is simply an extraordinary human being.

Waddles the Duck

Meeting David was not the first time my spirits had been lifted by a new friend. When I was about eight – feeling alone and not having the "best friends" that my sister, Ana, and brother Jay did – I set out to persuade my mother to let me have a pet duck. Ana's best friend was a black Siamese cat, Heidi; Jay's was an Alaskan Husky, King. So I, too, wanted a best friend of my own.

I hounded my mother for days about taking me down to the local feed store to glance at all the new arrivals of ducks and chickens. I was relentless in taking every opportunity to bring it up. After a few weeks of trying to ignoring me as I shuffled around the house, puppy dog eyes mourning and my head hanging down, my mother gave in. Although, most of the time, she was never one to cave, I must have been convincing, moping around the house for days until she finally drove me to the feed store on the west side of town.

Entering the store, the smell of animal feed and hay perfumed the air, giving it a country sensation. The store was filled with cages housing chickens, ducks, baby pigs and a few exotic birds. The noise of all the animals was deafening. As I wandered about this giant barnyard, I looked in the cages; I was hunting for the baby ducks. Passing by each cage, I could not see any candidates. But as I rounded the corner of an aisle, there it was: the duck cage, in the middle of the store, with a heat lamp hanging above it and the baby chickens mingled in with the baby ducks.

I looked into the cage hoping to find that one special duck. In the back of a large cage, there appeared

44

to be several chickens in a corner. I observed one of the baby ducks, pressed up against the side of the cage, fighting for its life. For some unknown reason, the baby chicks were pecking on it. The duck was bleeding from the neck area where all of his feathers had been pecked off and looking sad. How could that be? Why were these chickens so mean to that poor baby duck? My heart reached out to that little guy; he appeared to be an outcast – something I myself had felt many times. The desire to help this creature came over me at that exact moment; this little baby duck looked at me square in my eyes as if asking for help.

The store clerk appeared, asking, "May I help you with anything?"

"I would like the duck in the corner bleeding from his neck."

The clerk, chuckling, her mouth rising in one corner, responded by saying, "If that duck is being picked on by the others, that is a sign of weakness, and, most likely, it will not survive."

However, I wasn't fazed by his helplessness; my interest was in saving him. I knew this duck was the one. I felt in my heart that he needed someone to love and someone to love him. If those two elements were present in his life, I knew he would live. Despite the clerk's effort to persuade my mother to purchase a healthier duck, my mom knew I was determined to bring the unloved duck home with me.

After many failed attempts by the clerk, my mother, looking at me and observing my affinity for this helpless creature, purchased the duck. Anxious to hold

45

my new friend, I impatiently watched the clerk retrieve the bleeding duck from the cage where he was unwanted, handing him to me. In order to carry the duck home safely, I was given a small travel box, which I held close to my chest during our journey home. Keeping the lid on the box open so that we could bond during the tri, I lifted the duck out of the box and placed his face near mine. He looked up at me as if to acknowledge that he was now safe from harm.

It was important for him to know the love I had for him and to know no one would hurt him again. The more I held him, the happier he appeared to be. I knew he was the best choice. He was gentle and loving, quacking with joy.

Thinking that I could not just call him "duck," I knew he needed a name, one that would fit him well. I noticed that, as he walked around in the travel box on our way home, he seemed to waddle a bit. Holding the box, gazing at my buddy, I decided that, since he waddled, then that was what I would call him: Waddles.

Arriving home, I took Waddles inside the house, where my first order of business was to clean off his bloody neck and reassure him he was free from harm. Asking my mother for some clean rags and disinfectant, I set up a makeshift hospital to attend to Waddle's injuries. I kept telling him that everything would be OK now. I could sense that he knew what I was saying; his sense of safety effused from his body as he rubbed up against me. With each new moment together, our bond deepened.

After cleaning his neck and stopping the bleeding, I could see that he needed a place to bed down. There was no way I would allow him to sleep outside. I knew a perfect place to make a bed for Waddles: right next to mine. Locating a small box, one with low sides for easy access, I grabbed some old newspapers we had lying around and ripped several pages into long pieces for bedding.

Once the bedding was complete and ready, I picked up Waddles and placed him in it to acquaint the two. He thrashed around, pushing the shredded paper into one corner and then squatting down – a sign to me that he was content with his new home.

I sat there for hours next to his bed, conversing with my new friend, telling him how much fun we were going to have together. "I will take you everywhere with me, except for school, of course. Teachers are a bit fussy when it comes to animals at school; so, when I come home, we will hang out together."

When I arrived home from school every day, I found Waddles waiting for me at the door, just like a best friend would. Looking into his adorable little face, with that orange beak, I was saddened to think that, if I had not come along when I did to save him, he may have perished.

Waddles was someone I could spend time with as well as share my deepest thoughts and confide in. Although he could not speak my language out loud, I knew in my soul that Waddles was a part of me. He always put a smile on my face whenever I thought of him or when I arrived home to see him waiting for me to appear. I was always excited to see his wagging tail feathers and irresistible face as I entered the doorway each afternoon. (If I had possessed a ducktail, it, too, would have been wagging.)

He wasn't a duck, he was human – a living, breathing best friend. I cared for him, fed him, and spent endless hours just hanging out with him. Whenever I was watching TV, he insisted on nestling right next to me, eating popcorn out of the same bowl. If I were standing, I'd find Waddles lying between my feet. When I went to the local neighborhood grocery store, he was my companion, never wanting to leave my side.

At home, Waddles had his own potty box in the house and was trained to use it. When he wanted to go in or out of the house, he would gently tap on the back door. Any family member was happy to respond.

Waddles held a special place in my heart. I will never forget the love we had for each other. He was a true and dear friend; we shared a mutual love. But somewhere in my heart, I feared that the day would come when we would have to say goodbye.

One summer afternoon, during our fourth year together, Waddles was absent from his usual station by my side; it wasn't like him to hide or keep his distance from me. I went outside to see what my little duck friend was up to, checking his favorite hiding places. Still no sign of him. As I rounded the corner of the backyard patio, there was Waddles lying, dazed, struggling to keep his head upright. He tried to rise and run but could not, making crying sounds instead. This was not a good sign. Remembering that he loved to swim in his kiddy pool, I placed him in the water in hopes that he would recover. However, all he could do was flop around.

Unsure of what to do, I yelled for my mother, tears pouring from my eyes and sadness in my heart. My best friend was ill, and I was unsure how to fix what was wrong. My mom jumped into action, grabbed the blanket that Waddles loved to cuddle in, and wrapped him in it to comfort him. Before heading off to the hospital, my mother placed a call to the vet's office, informing them we were en route with our sick pet duck.

The initial response from the nurse on the other end of the phone was laughter.

"A duck? You want to bring in a duck?"

"Yes. It's my daughter's pet, and something is wrong. We will be right down."

My mother hung up the phone, yelled at me to get in the car, and we headed off in our 1956 Cadillac. Not wasting any time, or obeying any speed limits, my mom rushed Waddles to the animal hospital.

As we tore along the city streets to the vet, my heart sad and hurt, I cried.

"I can't believe I'm crying over a duck," my mom declared. But he wasn't just a duck; he was Waddles, who reigned supreme in heart. I felt searing pain for my stricken friend.

I kept praying to God, "Please let my best friend be OK. I promise not to be bad."

As we arrived at the hospital, I leaped from the car in a dead run holding Waddles, my mother pushing open the front door for me. Once we were inside, tears still pouring from our eyes, Waddles appeared unresponsive. I was reluctant to release Waddles to the doctor, for fear I would never see my cherished pet again. I couldn't lose my best friend; I couldn't!

As the vet pulled Waddles from my arms, he promised, "I will do the best I can to save your friend."

Although I was sure the doctor had done his best to fulfill that promise, the sadness in his face as he returned to the room foreshadowed the news that we had been dreading.

My mother asked, "Will Waddles be OK?"

All the doctor could do was shake his head as he struggled with the words, "No. He died while being examined."

My grief ran even faster down my cheeks, my heart aching because I had failed in my promise to protect my beloved friend always.

"I don't understand," my mother replied. "How did this happen? He seemed fine just yesterday."

"It was sunstroke."

"Sunstroke? But he has a kiddy pool," she objected. She clearly wasn't any more convinced than I was that Waddles wasn't coming back home.

"My best guess is that, in his older age, he may not have been able to climb over the edge of the pool. I am very sorry."

Feeling utterly lacerated, I asked the doctor if I could say my last goodbyes to my friend – alone. Granting my wishes, he escorted me to the examining room where Waddles lay still on the table as if he were taking a nap.

I held my friend for the last time, comforting him, holding him close to my face, and telling him that he had given me more love and companionship that I could ever hope for in a friend.

"Waddles, I will never forget you; there will always be a special place in my heart for you. God needed you more than I do, so be good and don't forget me. I love you."

A KISS TO REMEMBER

The memory of a special friend resurrected a transport of nostalgia for my duck Waddles. In 1972, my parents had sold our house in Richmond, California, a city located in the East Bay of San Francisco, home to Rosie the Riveter during World War II.

The family's sights were set on Petaluma, California, part of the North Bay sub-region of the San Francisco Bay Area, located 26 miles north of Richmond. This transition disrupted the family routine for a short time. The house had sold a few months prior to the end of the school year, I a sophomore and Jay a graduating senior. Not wanting to leave and transfer to Petaluma High School, we begged our parents to allow us to finish out the remainder of the school year.

Since my parents were hesitant to leave us behind with an acquaintance, our brother-in-law Cosmo, an Italian immigrant married to my sister Ana, offered a solution. A longtime friend and co-worker of his, Lorenzo, also an Italian immigrant, had an apartment in Oakland, California, where he offered us a place to bed down until graduation

Mom and Dad, feeling apprehensive, protective, and uneasy, knowing their nest would be separating, made a unanimous decision. They kept convincing each other that the separation, although short-lived, was the wise thing to do.

Commuting ten miles to Kennedy High School in Richmond from Oakland, alongside Jay, didn't seem all that bad. I was glad we had a car to share – a 1954

Chevy 210, two door hardtop purchased by our father. I was eager to complete the school year with Jay, and I wasn't yet ready to leave the only life I knew in Richmond.

On weekends, I traveled to Petaluma, spending time with family and kick-starting my transitional new life. Friendless, during my visits I would hang out at Cosmo's Delicatessen, which was gaining momentum and popularity, to consume time.

A neighbor of the Delicatessen was Walgreen's Drug Store. I would frequent the store for something to do. Having a love for music, I enjoyed acquiring the latest 45 record. One afternoon, the store's assistant manager, David Shaw, came by the deli for lunch. I was sitting in the back corner, talking to my sister, when she noticed David at the counter. Cosmo was assisting David with his order, when my sister jumped up and summoned him over to our table, introducing me to him.

Ana and David spoke about business and the upcoming summer. He was not an attractive man by any standards. A neatly trimmed beard, framing his unprepossessing face, complemented his short dark hair while highlighting his tall, medium build. There was a gentleness about him that was comforting. For sometime Ana had known David, who often came over on his lunch hour from his job next door.

Commuting back and forth on weekends was fatiguing. But once I had arrived, I enjoyed my time in Petaluma – time that helped me to get to know my surroundings. A few weekends passed. On Saturday, while spending time keeping up on the newest of tunes, I was in search for a new 45 record. After lunch at the

53

Deli, I ventured over to Walgreen's and combed their 45's clearance section. While I was flipping past each record, I heard a voice. Looking up, I noticed it to be David, asking if I was in need of any assistance, apparently using it as an excuse to initiate conversation.

Clearing his throat, he asked, "Can I take you to a movie or pizza one of these weekends when you're in town?"

Standing silent, I was a bit shocked, as this was the first time a boy had ever asked me out. Nervous and scared, I struggled to respond.

"Sure."

Next thing I knew, we had set a date for two weeks. Not sure of what to expect, I requested that we meet at the deli and have dinner at Shakey's Pizza Parlor in the same Shopping Center as the deli. At that point I wasn't sure if my sister had been trying to set us up or if he was aware this was my first date. But it didn't matter; something about him was plainly special.

Our meeting was a typical first date – small talk and learning about each other. David was a gentleman, opening the door, pulling out my chair, and letting me order first. I was still scared about how this night might end. Never before on a first date, I had nothing to compare it to. My body, reserved, had shifted into self-preservation mode.

As the date ended, David escorted me back to the deli, where my sister was closing up shop. While we stood in front of the store saying our goodbyes, David moved towards me. Although I thought at first that this was going to be a goodnight kiss, his arms opened as he gently hugged me.

"Thanks for a nice evening, Teresa, I sure hope we can do this again soon?"

Eyes aimed at the ground, I quietly responded, "It was a nice time David; maybe we can have a sandwich at the deli or catch an afternoon matinee."

"Sure."

I walked into the deli where my sister, waiting patiently for my return and ready to lock up, looked up at me, her eyes large with curiosity.

"So, how did it go?"

"Fine!"

I was not willing to offer any details. My reserve had surfaced again, commanding me to remain silent.

During the following weeks, my weekend visits afforded David and me time together for taking in a movie, or listening to popular tunes on his record player, or simply visiting.

I was beginning to take pleasure in David's company. He was stable, held a good job, was not experiencing with illegal drugs, and maintained a level-headedness that I liked. We discussed music, cars, and everyday life. Still, I was not harboring the desire for a steady relationship, which might detour me my career goals in law enforcement and mechanical repair.

Besides, dating was a territory I was unfamiliar with, and the unknown frightened me. My focus was firm, and I wasn't about to entertain any distractions.

One furiously rainy Friday afternoon, as I prepared to drive to Petaluma after school to keep a date with David, he called expressing concern for my safety and indicated he would come and pick me up. Knowing Monday was school day, David insisted on returning me to Oakland on the following Sunday.

This was the considerate side of David that I had grown to like. He always made me feel accepted and never an outcast for pursuing male-dominated careers.

While I sat in the apartment waiting for David to arrive, my brother Jay was preparing to go ice skating with his high school friend Joan Plant.

Discussing their plans, Jay asked, "Hey, Teresa, do you want to join us?"

"No, thanks, I'm going to Petaluma tonight. David is picking me up soon. Thanks anyway".

Keeping me company, Jay and Joan hung out while we waited for David to arrive around. Watching the clock approach the top of the hour, anticipating a knock on the door that was now considerably overdue, I tried calling his house. No answer. With no other means to contact him, all I could do was wait.

It was now past seven o'clock, with no signs of David. Jay and Joan were getting restless, eager to go ice skating, and insisted I accompany them. But this was not at all like David; standing me up was out of character for him. Worried that something might have happened to him, I started to pace back and forth in the apartment. When the phone rang, I vaulted up, my heart pounding. I ran to answer the phone.

"Hello, David?"

"No, Teresa, it's your mother; you need to come to Petaluma right away."

"Why? Is something wrong? David was to pick me up."

"Yes. David has been in an accident, and he is asking for you. Can you get here soon?"

In a panic, I slammed down the phone, grabbing my keys, running out the front door past Jay and Joan, never giving them any reason why I was in such a hurry – running as fast as my feet could take me. Jumping into the car, I drove as fast as I could towards Petaluma on Highway 101 heading north. The rain was heavy, and those vacuum wipers on the Chevy were no match to the downpour.

It was dark, the roadway flooded, and I was barely able to keep track of the white road lines. The forty four miles could just have seemed like a hundred. My head spun into every possible scenario as I listened to the wipers swishing back and forth.

Arriving it in one piece at the house, I was rushed back out into the rain by my mom, who ordered me into her car. Driving to the hospital, she was subtly trying to prepare me for something; it was hard to decipher what she wasn't telling me.

"Teresa, just be prepared to see David in a different light. He has been in an accident and from what I was told by Ana, it is serious."

A multitude of possible horrors were going through my head; it was difficult to focus on what my mother was saying. Arriving at the hospital, only a few miles from the house, I took a deep breath, exited the vehicle, and dashed toward the emergency side of Petaluma Hospital.

As my mother clung close to me for support while we walked through the double doors into Emergency, there was an aura of grey around her. As for me, a single tear began to roll down my face. I should have been bawling, but I was too numb to even think.

Walking towards the nurse sitting behind a desk checking in patients, I scanned the room, where I immediately spotted David's family – without a dry eye among them. With all the falling tears, it was raining as hard inside as outside.

"What is going on?" I inquired.

No verbal response from anyone – only emotional tears.

The emergency nurse came over inquiring, "Are you Teresa?"

"Yes," my voice cracking.

"Come with me. David is asking for you."

The nurse hurried me to a room noisy with the beeping of instruments and the scurrying of hospital staff. Now fear began to overtake me as I wondered *what is all this?* I had never been in an emergency room before, so this was all new.

As I rounded the corner, I saw David lying in a bed under a sheet, tubes and wires stationed all over him. I looked up and spotted one beeping machine displaying slender green lines that rose and fell ominously. As I gingerly approached his bed, he awoke for a moment, a smile appearing on his face. I could tell that he was happy to see me. When I reached his side, he extended his hand and softly spoke.

"Teresa, I am so glad you made it. I have little time. I want you to know I care for you, and whenever you hear the song *Last Kiss* [a favorite of ours] that's me watching over you."

Frozen, I feverishly asked myself *is this goodbye? Is he dying? No, it can't be!* It was at that moment, while holding his hand, that I felt the life depart his body. His strong hold on my hand slowly subsided as his hand fell away limply. Silence suffused the room as his body lay motionless. I didn't know what to do. I turned to the nurse for answers.

"He's gone. I am so sorry."

I, too, became motionless for a moment, then turned, running from the room to my mother, who was waiting for me.

"Are you OK, Teresa?"

"Let's go," I insisted.

I could hear David's family sobbing at the news of his passing. All the way home, I remained silent, shedding no tears and speaking no words. Losing a special friend was hard – a loss that brought back the feelings that I had held for my pet duck Waddles. These two losses may have differed, but my feelings were the same. I swore to never allow my heart to be broken again. Getting close to any living thing meant heartache, and I wanted nothing more to do with that experience. It hurt too much.

Days passed, and, refusing to show any emotions, I completely withdrew into my schoolwork for an entire week.

The following weekend I headed to Petaluma as usual, but now David's absence brought intense sadness and overwhelming feelings of loss. My special friend was no longer there to hang out with. Reading the local paper on that Saturday afternoon, I found David's obituary giving the date of his funeral. I wanted desperately to attend, but I had received word that David's sister was refusing my presence at the services, because she felt that it was my fault that her beloved brother had died driving to Oakland that night.

When the particulars of David's accident came to light, I learned that, while driving in heavy rain on his way to pick me up, David slid across two lanes leading into a curve with wet pavement under his tires, causing him to overcorrect and flip several times, the car landing on its roof. The driver of a passing tractor-trailer saw the headlights in the bushes, causing him to stop and render aid.

Assessing the seriousness of the accident, the truck driver radioed for help. A trucker on the other end answered the call for help, notifying the authorities and assuring that medical help was on the way. Time was of essence for David's life, and getting him medical attention was critical. Unfortunately, a couple of hours elapsed before David arrived at the hospital where he died.

David and his younger sister, Susan, had been close, and losing David set her into an emotional tailspin in which she desperately needed someone to blame for his death. Since David had been coming to pick me up, his death had to be my fault. Given her feelings, I abided by Susan's wishes by declining to attend the funeral.

During the following month, I refused to show any emotion over David's death, holding my feelings deep inside. I felt that expressing my sadness towards David's loss announced my feelings for him in a manner that was entirely too public for my comfort.

But my brother in-law kept telling me, "If you are sad, you need to cry. Let out your emotions; it will help the healing process."

Still, I refused and stood my ground – until one evening the family decided to go to dinner at the very same restaurant where David took me on our first date. Developments that evening proved more emotional than I could control.

As we arrived at the pizza parlor, the flood gates opened, and I thought for sure I would saturate my sister's car with tears. This was a difficult time for this 17 year old; but, once out of the car and heading into the restaurant, I regained my composure. Thinking back to my first date with David and reminiscing about our conversation causing the corners of my mouth to lift in joy, I knew he would watch over me throughout my life, because he had told me so by affirming our connection to the song *Last Kiss*.

The memory of our time together, briefly-lived, shall eternally live in my heart. And, so, from this moment on, whenever I hear *Last Kiss*, I'll remember David.

THE OUTCAST

If ever there was a true meaning of a tomboy, I was it. Not dainty or feminine, I never found dolls and fashion appealing. Instead, I embraced rugged outdoor activities and masculine adventures. Growing up in the '50s and '60s, I found my preferences to be a major challenge. From building friendships and battling with my mother, to self-acceptance and self-expression, I walked a tightrope of trying to "fit in" while being true to myself.

"Teresa, why can't you be like your sister Ana?" my mother would ask in desperation –
a question I heard on a near-daily basis while growing up.

Filled with frustration and sadness, I always replied, "Mom, I am not Ana. I am Teresa."

Unlike me, Ana was the epitome of the traditional female of my era. She was great at sewing, even making some of her own clothing. She was beautiful and smart, as well as enjoying the latest fashion trends, wearing make-up, and talking to boys. And, oh, how those boys liked talking to her! She was everything my mother knew and understood about what a girl should be. On the other hand, I enjoyed masculine activities like fishing, shooting, and bike riding. I liked getting my hands dirty and using them to tinker with and fix things. I took pride in my ability to understand the mechanics of how things worked, and I was good at it. I was everything my mother didn't expect and couldn't understand in a girl.

Ana and I could not have been more opposite growing up. It was her top priority for her outfit to look great; it was my top priority for my bike to be the shiniest. We shared a room and our morning routine played out as predictably as an endless video loop.

In Ana's case, it was always about her hair. First came the combing, then the ratting (that always took the longest) – handful after handful of hair yanked up and then pushed downward with a comb, creating a rat's nest effect.

This was followed by the dreaded hairspray. Aqua Net, contained in an obnoxious pink can, was her favorite choice. Placing the can high above her head, she would create a noxious cloud intended to coalesce into her hair. I would hear the *psst, psssst, pssssssssst* of the vile substance filling the bedroom, quickly followed by a sickly sweet odor and a fog rivaling San Francisco's worst. She must have used at least one can a day.

Then the yelling began.

"Ana, can't you spray that hair of yours in the bathroom? You're choking me to death!"

"Teresa, quit your complaining! I will finish in just a minute," she would huff, glaring at me.

"Yeah right; it only takes a minute to stop breathing," I would mumble, leaving our room for a breath of fresh air.

(I'm surprised more ladies from the sixties aren't experiencing COPD. With as much hairspray as was used back then, it's a wonder their hair didn't rebel.)

I have to admit though, in the end, Ana always accomplished the hairstyle she wanted and looked great. Achieving goals, no matter how we differed in our choices, was a characteristic we actually had in common, beyond being sisters -- although neither of us saw it at the time.

Ana thrived on femininity, and she was brilliant at it. I envied her, not because I wished to be like her, but because she was able to express herself as she wanted. Her lifestyle fit in with how society defined a lady and dictated what she should be. My style did not. I would wake up, brush my hair, and turn to put on pants and a t-shirt. But that was not an option. Slacks or Capris were considered "unladylike" and not allowed at school. Instead, I would mumble and grumble as I went to the closet to don my least intolerable blouse and skirt..

Society made it hard for a girl to have fun, particularly one like me. Forced to wear clothing that did not properly cover me, how could I? How could I climb the bars, swing on the swing, or play sports without revealing something best not exposed to sunlight?

When I think about those mornings getting ready for school with my sister, I see a picture of two extreme expectations: the unattainable ideals to which females are held, versus withering criticism for not meeting them. Ana worked hard to meet those standards; I rebelled against them. The primary difference was that she was accepted by society, whereas I was not. In our different ways, we were both profoundly affected by social norms.

As much as I wished otherwise, my mother never tired of trying to work her magic toward energizing my inner female.

"I'll make a lady out of you if it kills me" she would mutter under her breath as she sat curling my hair, much to my displeasure.

She would dress me up in skirts and blouses, buying an endless supply of tights that inevitably wound up with holes in the knees, grass stains, or mud splatters. It was a good thing I wasn't old enough to own a bra, or I may have been the first to burn one. (Somehow I doubt that burning a small Barbie shirt would have the same effect.)

Gifts were a sore spot, as in the occasion my parents gave me the newest Barbie, complete with cardboard house and a plastic Corvette. (Sadly, this dismal kit gathered dust in my closet.) Or the time when for Christmas I had asked – no, begged – for a toolset. I felt confident that my mom and dad had heard me and that I was going to finally get a gift I really wanted. Much to my disappointment and heartbreak, however, they gave me a set of hair curlers instead. I cringed, dying a little inside. Electric hair curlers were the perfect "tools" for Ana, not for me.

I longed for wrenches, drill bits, and screwdrivers. It wasn't that I was ungrateful for the gifts I had received, but my heart wasn't in them. I couldn't force myself to play with or use them, even though I felt bad knowing that there were so many other girls out there who would've loved them. But these girly, feminine things just weren't me. I couldn't pretend to be something other than myself. I felt unseen, unheard and misunderstood.

The gender stereotyping didn't stop with toys and clothing; it carried into the type of chores I was assigned.

My mother made sure to have me dust, vacuum, and clean the house with my sister on the weekends. After all, girls were to be homemakers.

I would have preferred cutting the lawn, trimming the bushes, or manicuring the yard. However, the outside chores were considered "manly" duties and assigned to my brother Gary, causing me considerable envy. My protest against housekeeping never swayed my mother. Her mission to turn this little tomboy into a lady put us at odds.

I now understand that my mother, as frustrating and unrelenting as she was in her quest for me to be a lady, was not being mean or evil. She was only staying true to what she had known as a girl growing up. Equipped with only her strong sense of what a woman should be, she was at a loss at how to respond to me. I imagined she was mostly driven by fear – fear about whether I would be accepted by society, whether I would be able to survive as an "outcast." No doubt she wondered that if she, my own mother, didn't know how to accept or understand me, how would society?

As for me, I felt enslaved within myself. With every protest against what my mother thought best for me – and against what society said I had to be – my discomfort only intensified and grew within me. My natural reserve kept me silent. I retreated into myself, my safe place – a place where I could be me.

Accordingly, connecting with other girls proved challenging for me. They and I never seemed to be on the same track. This disconnect was notably alarming. Was this the reason why Vivian had been so mean to

67

me? Did she dislike me because she couldn't connect with who I was and wanted to be? Had she found me threatening?

I found myself alone and ostracized. Why couldn't anyone accept me for who I was? Would I never find another human being with similar dreams?

Regardless, it was clear that this girl would not conform, no matter how hard my family or society pushed me. I felt trapped in a state that others were trying to change – felt as if I were inside a box pounding hard to escape. Searching for refuge, I turned to books and academics.

My favorite subject in school was American history, which included studying the American Civil War in the fourth grade. It was then that I learned about the life of Harriet Tubman, whose story intrigued me.

Tubman became famous as a "conductor" on the Underground Railroad during the turbulent 1850s. Born a slave on Maryland's Eastern Shore, she endured the harsh existence of a field hand, including brutal beatings. In 1849, she fled slavery, leaving her husband and family behind. Despite a bounty on her head, she returned to the South at least nineteen times to lead her family and hundreds of other slaves to freedom via the Underground Railroad. Tubman also served as a scout, spy, and nurse during the Civil War.

I looked up to Harriet, because of the hurt she had endured during her years as a slave – her family sold off and ripped apart, never to be seen again. Refusing to succumb to defeat, she turned around to help others. She proved that we can overcome obstacles, and, instead of submitting to hatred and anger, use our experience to pave the future.

I felt that Harriett and I had something in common: she needing to be free, and I feeling enslaved within myself and needing the exact same thing. She stood up for the oppressed – a condition that applied to us both. I was a conductor like Harriett – conducting my own escape from slavery.

Harriett appeared to be loner like me, her inner strength raging for release from slavery, while she maintained her true spirit no matter how cruelly life treated her. She never stopped trying to escape.

Every step Harriett took placed her life in danger; she never knew what lay around each corner – much like what a police officer faces each day on the beat. The more I learned about Harriet Tubman, the more my inner strength inspired me to be like her. Harriett was a strong, feisty and focused woman wanting to improve the lives of others. She was a true hero, one who suffered a great deal, yet harnessed her energy for only the positive. Harriet's tenacity was a real inspiration.

The story of Harriet Tubman's life made a lasting impression on me. I discovered that there were others in the world who were different, much as I was. Her story served as guidance for my future. I could relate to Harriett; I embraced and absorbed her life struggles; I grew curious in understanding what stirred her. What made her so fearless as to risk her life to save others she never knew? Her vision of freedom and a better life is truly worthy of emulation.

My desire to become a police officer mirrored what Harriett had become: a peacekeeper working to keep freedom alive while promoting a better life for others. She put her life on the line to free those in danger, much like the work of a police officer – work that resonated as a dream deep inside of me. I too was fighting to be free from danger – danger posed by those trying to change my destiny. My mentor, Harriet, had taken on the negative and reversed its direction for all whom she encountered, proving that we can empower others by our actions. And I was determined to live the same way.

If there is one understanding to be gained in life, it is the value of staying true to yourself, your dreams, and your goals, no matter the roadblocks. While fidelity to oneself can present its own challenges, we must never lose sight of the fact that we are in charge of our own destiny, steering it in the direction toward which we wish to travel. In that connection, I promised myself to stay focused and pursue my dreams, even against all odds. If one person as determined as Harriet Tubman can change history just by believing in herself, then any one of us can accomplish the same.

Even years beyond her time, Harriett Tubman helped me to believe.

VIVIAN THE BULLY

Two years before I learned about Harriet Tubman, I had already had an experience which made it easy for me to relate with her clients on the Underground Railroad...

Scared, breathing hard, and beginning to feel horrible, I knew exactly where to hide my small seven-year-old self. I quickly crawled into my special hiding place under the house, quiet as a librarian, and hunkered down. I knew it was only a matter of time before I would be a dead girl walking.

The neighborhood I lived in consisted mostly of households with school-age children like my siblings and me. We did not have computer games, cell phones, or Xbox to pass the time; instead, all of us would come together and play games: kick the can, hide and seek, or Olly-Olly Oxen Free. Playing these games kept us busy and out of trouble.

Included in our neighborhood play group was a girl named Vivian Martin, who was close to my age and clearly proud of her long golden hair and sapphire blue eyes. An only child who lived down the street from me, she was the daughter in a family that kept mostly to themselves.

This family was intolerably snobbish, as evident in the way Vivian carried herself as though the air around her was cleaner than mine. After all, the Martins did have all the modern devices, ranging from a garage door opener to a trash compactor, installed in their home. Vivian was the first girl on the block to have an electric curler, and she made certain that all of us kids in the neighborhood knew about it.

For reasons I couldn't understand, Vivian developed a disliking towards me. We were different in tastes, style and interests, but so what? These differences didn't bother the other girls living near me; why was she bothered so much? Whatever the case, she made it clear that she did not want to play with me. She took pleasure in calling me names and otherwise tormenting me.

I can still hear Vivian's voice as she chronically teased me:

"Look at Teresa, she looks and dresses like a boy. Who wants to play with her? Check out those skinny arms; she couldn't hurt a fly with those! Her family must be so poor. Just look at her clothes."

She was relentless, egging the other girls into ignoring me and hanging out with her instead. Unfortunately, the others went along with her. I can only assume they did it out of fear that they, too, would be left out or picked on. This bullying went on for months, which saddened me. So, I found other ways to occupy my time, playing mostly by myself.

One summer afternoon, I was out front riding my bicycle and loving the moment, when, to my dismay, Vivian appeared in my line of sight. She was skipping towards our house, her long blond hair bouncing up and down, wearing a big smile. I knew it couldn't be me she was in search of, since I would be the last one she would ever want to play with. The more I watched her, the closer she advanced. My heart sank, and my stomach knotted up. I was not in the mood for her name calling and derogatory comments.

Vivian kept on skipping, closing the gap between us, until we were standing face-to-face. Feeling uneasy, I was determined not to let my guard down. I could only imagine what her evil mind might be up to.

Vivian stood there for a second before saying, "Do you want to come over to my house and play?" Her voice was too sugary sweet for my liking.

She wants to play with me? I thought as I stood there in disbelief, my body frozen in place.

"Do you want to play with me!" she repeated, visibly annoyed.

Was she really talking to me? I looked up and down the street, but there was no one else around. Vivian Martin, my bully and tormentor for months, was now asking me to play with her; this day was getting weirder by the minute.

My curiosity was piqued. Why this sudden change of heart? I debated about whether I should go or not. But my eagerness to see the inside of her house outweighed my dislike for her. Everyone but me had been to Vivian's house at some point; I wanted to see for myself all the newest gadgets that Vivian so often bragged about.

"Um, okay." I finally answered.

As we walked the half-block to Vivian's house, I asked her, "Where are Lisa and Jenny?"

"They're on a camping trip," she answered.

"What about Jessica and Barbara?"

"Don't you think I would be playing with them instead of you if I could?" Her words stung. Why was she so mean and hurtful to me?

"I would ask Billy, but my mom doesn't want me to have boys over." She looked away from me. "Even if you act and dress like a boy, you're still a girl."

Of course! How silly I was to have thought she might be having a change of heart. She was desperate for a play companion, and I was it, the bottom of the barrel for her. As an only child, she probably so disliked playing alone that she could bring herself to play with me.

My face flushed hot as anger swelled within me. She was a mean, catty girl. I resolved to see the inside of her house and leave as quickly as possible. Any thought or hope that I could ever like or be friends with Vivian had been demolished. I was done with her. A feeling of strength seemed to grow in me. I no longer wished for acceptance from Vivian, and I felt exhilarated.

Arriving at her house, we were greeted by her mother, Marsha, who offered me some milk and cookies. I politely accepted. (How could I turn down fresh milk and cookies?) Mrs. Martin appeared pleased to see Vivian and me playing together. She had no clue as to what a brat and bully her daughter was – or else she was in plain denial.

We went upstairs to Vivian's room, which was something out of *Better Homes and Gardens,* with pretty pink walls, fluffy curtains and dolls of every description on display along with a white canopy bed with matching fringe.

After feasting my eyes on every little detail of her room, I was going to politely excuse myself. Instead – motivated more by curiosity than any wish to cozy up to Vivian – I heard myself asking her, "What do you want to play?"

Her response was immediate. "Let's play beautician."

This was more of an order than a suggestion. She didn't care what I wanted to play; I was only there for her entertainment. Again, that strange near-electric feeling of strength come over me.

"OK." Even though I had zero interest in playing this sort of game.

"You will pretend to be the beautician, cutting my hair," Vivian instructed, as she handed me a pair of scissors and a comb. She sat down and flipped her long, thick golden blonde hair towards my face.

"Now, beautician, cut my hair, and make sure you comb it out afterwards."

I couldn't believe I was doing this: playing with Vivian – beautician, of all things! All I could hear was the sound of the scissors in my hand. *Snip! Snip! Snip!* My heart began beating harder as my anger rose. *Snip! Snip! Snip!* Only. . . I wasn't pretending. I was getting even. I had had enough of the bullying from Vivian and her evil ways. *Snip! Snip! Snip!* Tired of her finding ways to keep my friends from playing with me and playing only with her. *Snip! Snip! Snip!* Of her thinking that my family was beneath her. *Snip! Snip! Snip!*

Finally I stopped, took a breath and stepped back to admire my work. I wondered how she'd feel now, with her perfect golden locks cut off at her neckline.

Thank goodness there was no mirror in Vivian's room, or else I would never have been able to accomplish this glorious triumph. With the benevolence that visits all who have achieved justice, I found my anger receding – and reality setting in.

While it felt great to get even with Vivian, I knew I was going to be in big trouble. Unlike the Martins, who thought their daughter could do no wrong, my parents had the nasty habit of holding me accountable for my actions.

"Well, it's been fun, but I have to go home. It's getting late."

"Wait! You didn't comb it yet!"

My feet were already off and running. I was half way down the stairs when I heard Vivian start screaming in hysterics. I was out of her house like a tornado, running as fast as my legs could carry me, *guilty* written all over my face. I could not believe what I had just done. No doubt, both Vivian and her mother were now aware that Vivian's prized blonde hair that once hung to her waistline was now lying in chunks on the floor.

Scared, breathing hard, and already starting to feel remorseful, I went to my special hiding place under the house. Secure in my refuge, I could hear every sound made inside the house. Suddenly, I could hear loud footsteps on our front porch, followed by quiet exhausted sobs. The doorbell rang repeatedly, accompanied by loud knocking; someone wanted in desperately. I knew it had to be Vivian's mother, coming to give my mother what-for. I wondered what Mrs. Martin thought of me now. Probably wanted her milk and cookies back?

I could hear the whole scenario playing out: my mother's footsteps as she approached the door, the knob turning, the slight squeak of the door opening, and my mother's voice

"Can I help –"

Before she was even able to finish her sentence Vivian's mom began yelling in a shrill voice. "Look what your daughter Teresa did to my Vivian's beautiful blonde hair! She cut it all off!"

My mother was flabbergasted. "Marsha, I apologize. I don't know what would ever make Teresa do such a thing."

"Well, I want her punished for this! And she is never allowed in our home again!"

"I doubt that that will be a problem."

Was there a drop of sarcasm in my mother's voice?

"However, I assure you I will get to the bottom of this, and Teresa will be properly dealt with."

There was a moment of silence before I heard footsteps leaving.

"Humph! Come on, Vivian," Mrs. Martin huffed.

The door slammed. I heard my mom taking a few deep breaths.

"Teresa Marie!" She began calling out my name. "Teresa Marie, get out here right now!" I sank deeper into the dirt beneath me.

"You better come out now or your punishment will only be worse!"

I was bound and determined to remain silent. After all, my mother didn't know if I was in the house hiding or at a friend's house avoiding the inevitable. After hearing her voice, I figured it was best to stay in my cubbyhole until her temper cooled a bit.

After about two hours huddled in a mess of tears, snot, guilt, and fear underneath the house, I heard a stirring above me. My older brother, Jay, had arrived home; the moment he entered the house, my mom was on him.

"Jay, where is your sister Teresa?"

"I don't know. What happened? Is she okay?" Worry in his voice.

"She decided to cut off little Vivian Martin's hair, that's what happened!" I could hear the agitation in her voice.

I let out the tiniest of groans. I was a horrible person. I had done an evil thing. Everyone was going to hate me now. If ever there were a situation calling for the razor strop, this was it. I was toast.

"What? Really! Well, Vivian isn't very nice."

"Jay! That isn't the point! I know you know where your sister would be hiding. Tell me where she is right now!"

I sucked in my breath. Mom was right. If anyone would know where I was hiding, it was Jay.

"I don't know, Ma. Seriously."

I let my breath out; he hadn't squealed on me.

"Yeah, right," My mom sighed. "If you're hungry, there are sandwiches in the fridge."

My stomach growled at the thought of food.

"Thanks, Ma."

About 15 minutes later I could hear footsteps outside approaching my special spot. My heart started pounding. Was it my mom? Even worse, had Mrs. Martin found me?

"Hey, I know you're under there. You really should come out now if you know what is good for you." It was my brother Jay.

"Go away," I whispered

"Ma is looking for you, but you know that already." I could hear a note of sympathy in his voice.

"Leave me alone," I said quietly.

I had a plan, and I was sticking to it. I was going to wait until dad got home. As Daddy's little girl, I knew the punishment from him wouldn't be as bad as my mother's. Going into the lion's den wasn't a good choice just yet.

"Did you really cut off her hair?" Jay snickered.

"Yes."

"Well, she *is* mean, and it is just hair. It will grow back."

Tears rolled down my cheek. My brother didn't hate me. Maybe I wasn't evil after all.

I listened to his footsteps as he walked away.

After what seemed an eternity, I finally heard the garage door open. I knew it was my father coming home from work. I had to get to him before my mom did. I timed my exit from my hiding place perfectly, grabbing my father the second he was out of the car.

As I began to explain what happened, I was speaking so fast he couldn't understand a word I was saying. Suddenly, the door to the house opened; it was my mother, wearing that famous angry look on her face.

I would not let go of my father's leg. I was hanging on for my life. He had to save me, and, by the grace of God, he did so. Furthermore, by that time my mother had calmed down quite a bit. It was the moment of truth; my parents wanted to know why a shy and quiet person like me would do such a terrible deed.

I confessed to cutting Vivian's hair.

"She was the one who wanted to play beautician, and I was just giving it the full effect. I'm tired of her; she is always bullying me and trying to make me feel poor and ugly. So I gave her a taste of her own medicine."

After pleading my case, I could see a small smirk growing out of the corner of my mother's mouth. Did she secretly agree?

Ultimately, I was spared the razor strop, and no one hated me as I had feared. I was on restriction for a month: no playing outside, no TV, no telephone, and no playing with Vivian. (That last one was a real heartbreaker. I wasn't about to ever set another foot in Vivian's house again – a loss I was sure I could handle.)

Vivian never bullied me again.

DRAFTING ISN'T FOR YOU

Harming Vivian the bully was out of character for me. I knew it was the wrong thing to do, but, at the moment, it appeared to be my only solution. I really don't know what came over me, and I still have mixed feelings about it.

Moving to Petaluma would prove to be a turning point even though it would be short-lived. I had the entire summer to acclimate to living in our new home, a six bedroom, three bath, three car garage, two-story house in a new housing development on the East Side of Petaluma.

My mother worked hard to make our new house a home, for all of us. Much of the old furniture did not find its way to Petaluma; my mother and father wanted to make the move to Petaluma a new start with new home furnishings. The move was hard on us all; for me, being a shy person, I wasn't sure if I could fit in. This was new territory for me. The move was my first time experiencing a new beginning, in a town where I was a stranger to all. I was skeptical.

As the first summer in Petaluma came to a close, it was now time for me to transition into a new school, Petaluma High. Not knowing a soul, I gave it my all. I was accustomed to an overcrowded school, where the whites were the minority, not a majority. Petaluma High's campus was small, with a total student population of around 1600. Transferring from Kennedy High School, where the student population approached 5,000, presented quite a culture shock.

The riots we left behind were a mere topic of conversation, not a reality in this small country town. I felt safe knowing I could roam the school halls without the fear of being beaten up. It didn't take me long to meet classmates who would become lifelong friends. Although I had lived in Richmond for sixteen years, I now was finding old friendships fading into memories of the past.

Being an individual focused on what I wanted out of life, I had stayed true to my dreams, never wavering in spite of the racial turmoil which constantly distracted me. But my junior year in Petaluma was going to be different; all the rioting I had experienced just thirty three miles away now seemed to be separated by an ocean, allowing me to breathe a little easier.

Still, it took me weeks to stop waiting for trouble to break out – out of habit, not because there was a reason for caution. Moving to Petaluma was like going to an island or different country, because people here were friendly and carefree. Walking down the street, people would wave at me to say hi. It was the flavor of living in a small town, and I loved it.

My junior year at Petaluma High gave me the opportunity to grow as a person and to make footprints towards my personal goals. I developed a circle of friends and signed up for an art class to expand on my creative side. I loved drawing and photography and attending art class, both of which helped stir my desire to create.

My art teacher, Mr. Hawkins, possessed a passion for teaching – evident by the way his face beamed like a bright light every day during class. Art was one of my favorite classes; I let my mind wander, making creative dreams come true – on paper to boot.

Mr. Hawkins, intrigued that I was so set on pursuing male-oriented professions, and I would spend time before or after class chatting about my future goals. He observed the smile on my face and could hear my voice of passion when I spoke about my dreams.

One afternoon as I was heading to art class, Mr. Hawkins stopped me in the hallway, asking if he could speak with me and stepped some distance down the hallway so that other students couldn't hear our conversation. At first, I was concerned as to the matter of this meeting, but, after he explained his reasoning, his intent was clear.

"Teresa, I know you want to pursue law enforcement and mechanics, so I think it would be wise of you to enroll in drafting next semester."

"You think I will need drafting in both careers?"

"I have given it a lot of thought since you and I spoke about it last, and I think it would be a good class to take. You will most likely need drafting knowledge for accident scene investigation and for reading schematics as a mechanic. So be sure to enroll."

Wow. I was excited to hear that a man was in favor of my goals and was offering me guidance towards my future. I knew this was a good sign.

The semester enrollment period arrived, and I did as Mr. Hawkins had advised; I enrolled in drafting. After submitting my enrollment requests, there was a waiting period before learning if I was accepted or not, which depended on how many students enrolled.

Arriving at school early was my daily routine. I parked my car, headed to my homeroom class and settled in before the ringing of the morning bell. Soon the day arrived when I would learn the fate of my next semester class assignments. My homeroom teacher, Mrs. Stonehage, handed out their next semester classes to every student.

When I received my schedule, I found a note attached to the sheet which read *Your request has been denied,* expressing no explanation as to why. Arriving at my art class that afternoon, I handed Mr. Hawkins the note.

Mr. Hawkins left the classroom and immediately marched to the counselor's office to inquire as to why I had been denied. Little did I know, this was about to start a battle of the sexes – not because I was looking for a fight but because I was just following what my art teacher advised me to do.

Mr. Hawkins returned to the classroom and summoned me to his desk.

"Teresa, it appears that the reason you were denied, is that the drafting teacher, Mr. Pallozari, will not allow any girls in his class. I have asked for a meeting with the Principal tomorrow and I will let you know how it goes."

I didn't know what to say to Mr. Hawkins for sticking his neck out for me. I stood there, shocked that my teacher was standing up for me and my dreams. In my eyes, he was the greatest teacher on earth. No one had ever gone out of his way for me before. This was a first for me.

The next day at school I was eager to learn the outcome of the meeting between Mr. Hawkins and Principal Lightfoot. I knew that in time I would learn of my chances of being allowed into Mr. Pallozari's drafting class.

When I arrived at my art class that afternoon, I was hoping Mr. Hawkins would shine some light on the situation. Entering the classroom, Mr. Hawkins waved me up to his desk.

"So, how did the meeting go today with the Principal?"

"Teresa, you're in. I had to persuade the principal as to why you needed the class, and I explained that I was the one who encouraged you to enroll. At first, he sided with Mr. Pallozari; but I explained that we are an educational institution and that if we are not doing our best to educate, then we shouldn't be here. It is not a matter of male or female; all students should have the privilege to learn."

"Wow! Mr. Hawkins, I don't know how to thank you. I appreciate your taking the time to defend my reason for taking drafting, and you are the best. Thank you so much."

"Just make me proud, Teresa. That is all I ask. You are a good student, and you deserve the chance."

My first day in drafting class was not as happy an occasion as I had been hoping for. Mr. Pallozari was not at all amused by my presence in his classroom. He was clear from the get-go that his feelings at having a female in his class were decidedly negative.

"Welcome class, I want to start off by saying that we are forced to have a female student in our class against my wishes. This is the first time in all my years of teaching here that a female has been allowed in drafting class."

His eyes zeroed in on me as I sank a little into my chair.

"I hope you can keep up with the other students, Teresa, because I will give you no special treatment."

Sitting in my seat and feeling smaller than a snail, I was at a loss for words. I felt as if I had been hit by a baseball bat, right smack in the face. I didn't remember asking for any special treatment, and I was here to learn, not goof off.

I had made the Honor Roll every semester so far, and I was hoping that this one would be no different. During the following weeks, I worked hard, studying my assignments until my eyes struggled to stay open. Nevertheless, my work in drafting class wasn't getting the best of grades.

I couldn't figure out why. But I made friends with two male students in that class. The others seemed to treat me as if I had cooties. I compared my work with my two friends to see if maybe I was missing something, but that was not the case. I even asked them if they knew why my work was receiving poor grades. They seemed unable to suggest any reasons. If they knew, both were afraid to offer up the truth.

I was frustrated. I knew I had this – certainly not as an A-student, but at least a B or B-, not constant D's. Although I did not let this sentiment get me down, I couldn't understand the basis of Mr. Pallozari's dislike for me, other than that I was a female changing the décor of the class.

The semester was ending and, boy, was I glad – not because I disliked the class but because the teacher disliked me and had made every attempt to let me know.

On the last day of class, Mr. Pallozari handed out our final grades. Since my last name begins with an *A*, I was first to receive my report card. Mr. Pallozari walked over to my desk, swinging his arm, and, with my card in hand, put it almost directly in my face.

"I hope you enjoy it," he said with a smug look on his face.

After grabbing my report card, I knew this would not be good. I slowly brought the paper up to my face and, with my insides churning, I gave my grade a glance. My eyes opened wide as my eyebrows popped up. I couldn't believe it! How did I deserve a D-?

After passing out the report cards to all the other students, Mr. Pallozari walked up to the front of the class, dismissing everyone. Shaking my head and mumbling my frustration under my breath, I stepped past Mr. Pallozari. While a few of the cootie boys were eagerly chatting with him, I glared at the malevolent chauvinist.

"I knew you couldn't pass this class, Teresa. I do truly hope you enjoy your grade." The cootie boys snickered in agreement.

My sharp, hard-to-restrain Italian temper almost surfaced, but, counseling myself, *Wait, what I am doing here?* I turned, took a deep breath and replied, "Mr. Pallozari, a grade is just an opinion. I came in this class to learn drafting, and I am leaving this class with the same knowledge that the other students have gained. You cannot take that away from me. So you have a nice day."

I turned, walked out of the class with my shoulders back, head high, and feeling sassy. I'm sure Mr. Pallozari wanted me to cry, thinking this is what girls do. Well, not this girl. Firing back felt good; I felt empowered. I had refused to allow him the pleasure of seeing me sad or angry, tears flowing down my cheeks. Feeling his shock and disappointment as I took the last step out of his classroom, I couldn't help but smirk.

While Mr. Pallozari had been a thorn in my side, Mr. Hawkins was my hero. With his remarkable foresight, he knew that I would need the skills I learned in drafting class. And he fought to ensure that I received them.

I did not make the Honor Roll that semester. What I did make, instead, was a path for other female students to follow in my footsteps. But I was not finished!

YOU CAN'T BE A MECHANIC OR A COP

I couldn't do it. I couldn't say something on paper that wasn't true. It killed me to spell out the word -

S-e-c-r-e-t-a-r-y.

Harriett Tubman appeared a loner like I was – her inner strength raging for release as a slave, maintaining her true spirit no matter how hard life was. She never stopped trying to escape.

For Open House, occurring early in my fourth grade year, the theme was "What do you want to be when you grow up?" Mrs. Wheeler, my fourth grade teacher, had advised the class that we would be sharing our future hopes and dreams during that event. I was ecstatic. I knew exactly what I wanted to be when I grew up, and I couldn't wait to share my dreams with my school and the parents of my peers.

During Open House, all around the perimeter of the classroom stood a student, dutifully underneath the job he or she wishes to acquire. All my peers were smiling and excited to be sharing this topic with their parents. I, on the other hand, was feeling miserable as my thoughts went back to earlier in the week and the events that led to the lie hanging above my head.

It all started when my teacher, Mrs. Wheeler, asked us to put away our books and pull out a piece of lined writing paper – the kind with two wide solid lines with a dotted line down the middle to show where the center was.

"Children, as you know, the school will host an Open House next week, and I would like for you to write what it is you wish to be when you grow up. When completed, turn your papers in to me before you leave."

This was exciting; I knew exactly what I would put down. I grabbed my piece of writing paper and looked for a sharp pencil to ensure my words stood out. Not one pencil had a point, so I rushed to the pencil sharpener, pushed in my pencil, cranking the handle. That point had to be perfect.

Satisfied with my pencil's sharpness, I hurried back to my desk. While a few of my fellow classmates were still trying to decide their fate, I began to write in as perfect penmanship as I could.

I want to be a police officer, and I want to be a mechanic when I grow up.

I picked up the paper, giving it a fleeting look to make sure that I had stayed within the lines. Yep, it looked perfect and, thanks to my sharp pencil, the words stood out.

With satisfaction at finishing the assignment, I delivered my paper to Mrs. Wheeler's desk. Returning to my desk, I heard Mrs. Wheeler call out to me, "Teresa, could you come here, please?"

She must have read my paper and wants to congratulate me on some great choices for my future.

"Yes, Mrs. Wheeler?"

"Teresa, I want to discuss what you wrote. You want to be a police officer and a mechanic?"

91

I didn't understand why she seemed surprised.

"I'm sorry; women may not be police officers or mechanics. Women can be secretaries, nurses, housewives, or even matrons, but not the two you have chosen here." Mrs. Wheeler responded.

My heart sank; this was not going at all like I thought it would. None of those types of jobs appealed to me.

"But, Mrs. Wheeler, I wrote what I want to be –"

"Teresa, I have no other choice. If you do not change your paper to something more in line with what women can accomplish, I will have to flunk you."

Flunk me? For telling the truth? I was devastated. I looked at Mrs. Wheeler, hoping I might be able to change her mind; but, from the expression on her face, I knew she was set on restricting me from even thinking it was possible.

How could this be true? I held high hopes for my future, and it was not what society was dictating to me. Standing in front of Mrs. Wheeler, frozen in time, I couldn't believe this was happening. First, my mother negated my desires, and now my teacher was doing the same.

"You may return to your desk now."

The conversation at an end, I felt hurt and defeated, retreating to my seat. Sitting muted and confused, I retrieved a new piece of writing paper. I saw Mrs. Wheeler watching me out of the corner of her eye. I started to write:

What I want to be when I grow up is a...

I could barely do it. I couldn't stand to write something that wasn't true. It devastated me to spell out the nauseating word –

S-e-c-r-e-t-a-r-y

This time around it took me forever to complete the assignment. Caving in, I submitted a paper I emphatically did believe in – and in my handwriting at that! This time Mrs. Wheeler gave me her approval. Eyes crinkling with satisfaction, she crumpled up my original paper and flipped it into the trash.

I left the classroom in horror, seething and anguished, my head hung low. My three-mile walk home seemed in slow motion, while I continued trying to understand why I couldn't be a police officer or a mechanic – why a woman, specifically, could not pursue these fields. This denial felt so unfair.

Having arrived home, I couldn't change out of my "girly" clothes fast enough. They were a reminder to me of the oppression I felt. This leaden weight around my heart threatened my very breath. The clothing, the rules, the constant denial of female potential was cruelly suffocating me.

I found my mother doing house chores, another shining example of what a woman should do, and I was instantly irritated.

"Teresa, is everything all right? You look like something is wrong."

My head rising up, the floodgates opened. Although I was normally quiet, the injustice of being forced to lie about my dreams in order not to be flunked was too much to bear.

"Mom, why is it so many people are against what I want to be when I grow up? Every time I mention that I want to be a cop and a mechanic, people tell me NO. Today Mrs. Wheeler, asked us to write down what we want to be when we grow up for the upcoming open house, so I did. I did exactly as she asked. I know what I want to be, but after I wrote it down, she called me to her desk and told me that I cannot be a police officer or a mechanic – and that if I did not change my choices, she would flunk me."

"Well, Teresa, I guess it is because women aren't mechanics or cops. Do you know any? I don't. So these professions you are dreaming of –"

"This is not a pipe dream! Can't you understand that? These two careers are what I want to follow, not what you or any teacher wants. And don't you think it was unfair for her to force me to go along with her ideas?"

"Life isn't fair. Get used to it. Sounds like Mrs. Wheeler was trying to save you from disappointment."

There was no point in arguing. I was never going to convince my mom otherwise. It didn't surprise me. I had known for some time that my mom was not a fan of my plans. Nevertheless, her unsupportiveness still hurt me every time.

When Open House finally arrived, I found myself standing rigidly under the hated secretary label, feeling the humiliation of a slave at auction.

I was there not to exhibit my defeat, but to protest it. As parents passed by reading our papers, I asserted that I had been forced to write secretary as my career choice, in spite of my real desire to be a mechanic and police officer.

Mrs. Wheeler thought I was being defiant. She and my mother proceeded to talk about me as though I weren't standing right there and couldn't hear every word. It took everything in me to keep still, but I knew that speaking up would land me in hot water. Instead, I listened and kept to my task at hand, telling every passerby that the words written on the paper above my head were lies. I stood defiantly, arms crossed and chin jutted, determined that truth would be heard by anyone who would listen.

"Teresa seems very upset."

"Mrs. Wheeler, you told Teresa that if she didn't change what she wanted to be when she grew up, which she keeps insisting is a police officer or a mechanic, you would flunk her. Of course she is upset. My daughter is very strong-willed."

Interesting, I thought. *Is my mother standing up for me?*

"I was only trying to protect her from disappointment, not to be mean. She is such a great student, and she loves school. I wanted her to know her dream jobs are out of reach."

95

"Welcome to my world. I couldn't agree more."

Nope, she wasn't standing up for what I wanted; in fact, she agreed with Mrs. Wheeler. My heart sank as I crossed my arms, curling my lips, holding back my frustration.

"It isn't that Teresa is being defiant; she just refuses to stop expressing her passion and protests every time I try to protect her from reality. But there seems to be no changing her mind."

"I see."

"Well, I hope she knows she has a tough road ahead of her."

With that, their conversation ended. I felt hurt, angry – even betrayed – that neither of them could or would support me in my endeavors. It was isolating and confusing.

I know that, down deep, both my mother and teacher weren't being cruel or vindictive about their beliefs; they were judging me on the basis of their upbringing, following society's expectations.

This was a huge blow to my self-esteem. But in the back of my mind, I knew I would succeed one day with or without the help of others.

This was my dream, not theirs. Without a doubt, it would come true.

An image of Teresa at the beginning of her law enforcement career in 1977.

MY LAW ENFORCEMENT CAREER BEGINS

Succumbing to Mrs. Wheeler's doubts would have meant sabotaging my future dreams. Pursuing a career in law enforcement took center stage with my every breath...

One warm summer day, I was working day shift at a dog chow plant in accounts payable, the very type of job from which I had vowed to keep my distance. While eating my lunch, reading a large display add in the newspaper, I learned about an opening for Reserve Deputies at the local Sheriff's Department. Further reading revealed an outline of the qualifications and where to apply. Ripping the ad from the paper, I decided to apply after work.

Leaving work, I headed straight for the sheriff's department patrol division to apply. Grinning wide, my face beaming, I entering the Patrol office, where to the left, just inside the doorway, sat a hot-pants-clad teenage receptionist. I wasted no time on small talk, immediately expressing my reason for being there: to apply for Reserve Deputy. Excited about this opportunity, I quickly filled out the application and turned it in to the receptionist before heading home

Life was beginning to fall into place. My dream of becoming a police officer just might come true. Fighting crime instead of fighting paper cuts was more in line with how I imagined my future.

Waiting for the Sheriff's Department to call, I was suffused with anticipation. The process wasn't nearly as quick as I had been hoping for, but my possible shot at a position made the wait worthwhile. Two agonizing months passed before I heard from the Sheriff's Department.

One afternoon the phone rang.

"Hi Teresa, this is Lt. Smith at the Sheriff's Department. I am calling to let you know you have made the first cut in applying for Reserve Deputy. We are conducting interviews this coming Saturday, and I am hoping you can make it."

After hanging up, I stood motionless, letting this moment sink in. *Oh my goodness*, I thought. *I might get to be a reserve deputy! Yesss!*

This was the moment I had been waiting for, a chance at being a police officer. Both careers were taking shape, first as a mechanic and now a chance at being a Deputy. I had not yet secured a position with the Sheriff's Department, but I was going to do everything in my power to do so. My focus instantly shifted to passing the interview. A million questions were circling my brain. The only problem was that I had no idea what to prepare for.

Waiting for Saturday brought the longest five days of my life. When that morning finally arrived, I entered the Sheriff's Department and noticed six somber-looking males in the hallway, some sitting in chairs and others milling around anxiously. Unaware of who my contact might be, I asked one of the males if he was waiting to be interviewed. He confirmed that all six were there to interview for Reserve Deputy.

A door in the center of the hallway opened. Entering the hallway a tall uniformed man, whose shinny boots caught my eye, announced, "If you are here to be interviewed for Reserve Deputy, please take a seat in one of the chairs here, and someone will soon call your name."

As we were called in one by one, each applicant went through the door but failed to come back out. I supposed the interviewers wanted to avoid our asking interviewee's questions pertaining to the process. I was paralyzed with nerves, praying this opportunity would become a reality. Those who had gone ahead of me were now all absent from the hallway. I was the only remaining interviewee. My heart fluttered as my blood pressure hit the limit.

Finally the door opened, and I heard my name echoing in the hallway. Breathing deep, I rose and entered the room. It was rather large, featuring a long maple table surrounded by four men in plain clothes. To my right sat a short, balding, fair skinned man, separate from the others, staring at me. Not sure what to make of this intimidating scene, I was nervous. A tall fair-haired man at the head of the table smiled at me warmly, gesturing for me to sit down directly across from him.

"Welcome. Before we get started, can we offer you some water?"

"No, thank you. I'm fine."

Then the questions began.

"I am Lt. Stone. You are Teresa Aquila, is that correct?"

"Yes, Sir, that is correct."

100

Whew! At least that was an easy question I knew I got right.

The officer who sat to the left of Lt. Stone spoke next.

"Teresa, I am Joe Howard. Nice to meet you. Why do you want to be a Reserve Deputy?"

Another easy question, one I could answer clearly:

"Well, ever since I was in first grade, when a police officer visited my school, I knew in my heart that that is what I want to be. He was confident, he loved his line of work, and he wasn't out to just arrest people but to work with communities to help improve their quality of life. It profoundly affected me. I too, wish to help communities, in a similar way – as well as to learn about and contribute to law enforcement."

Lt. Stone took on the next question.

"Teresa, have you ever been in trouble with the law?"

"No, just my mother, and, believe me, if you can survive her, the law would never need to intervene."

This elicited chuckles all around. I was becoming more relaxed, and my confidence was building.

Now it was Joe Howard's turn.

"Have you ever stolen anything that did not belong to you?"

"Now that is a tough question. When I was about five years old, my mother owned a cash register piggy bank. It accepted only quarters, and when it reached $25.00 the bank opened. I had been eyeing a cap gun at our local grocery store, just down the street from our house, and I really wanted it. I figured a way to remove some of the quarters before the bank hit the $25.00 mark – only removing enough to pay for the gun.

"Piling the stolen quarters in my right pants pocket and leaving the house as fast as I could, I ran down to the store. The one thing I forgot was to cover up the evidence. I proudly placed the quarters on the store's counter to pay for the gun and ran back home to play with it. Not expecting my mother to have noticed the missing quarters, when I got home, I found my mother standing murderously on the front porch, arms crossed and eyes squinting menacingly.

"In my excitement to get the gun, I had foolishly left the bank on the bed, clear evidence that it had been broken into. Once I saw that look, while holding the gun, I squealed about my little crime to my mother. As a result, I was punished in an unusual way: I had to return the toy and explain to the store's owner why I was returning it. It was painfully embarrassing to hand back the toy and spill my guts that I was a thief.

"Needless to say, I never did anything like that again; I actually laugh a little looking back at my fear that taking a few quarters from my mother at age five could jeopardize my chances of becoming a deputy. But, hey,

I'm not going to hold back anything. I want this more than I can explain."

The questioning continued, covering character, honesty and ability to handle a variety of situations. I was feeling confident about my answers; they were real and honest.

I had nothing to hide. All my life I had behaved in school, held good grades, made the honor roll many times and, above all, obeyed the law – always. My parents had brought me up that way. Knowing what I wanted out of life early helped me to stay focused. Never having the desire to try illegal drugs of any kind, I instinctively knew that doing so could hurt my future in law enforcement.

Instantly relieved when my interrogation was over, I was asked to leave the room. Having been instructed to exit through a different door and to wait in a separate hallway, I now knew where the other applicants had gone after their interviews. I joined them.

Half an hour passed before the door to the interview room opened again. It was Mr. Howard, who announced, "If I call your name, we thank you for your time and applying. However, it was not the right fit for our department."

I felt my stomach leap into my throat. *Please don't call my name, please don't call my name, please don't call my name,* I repeated over and over in my head like a record skipping. To my utter relief, Mr. Howard excused two of the group and I was not one of them. I could breathe again.

There were four left. We were then asked to head over to a door reading *Polygraph Testing*. I instantly saw what the next round of the interview would entail. It was an old-fashioned polygraph machine, the type for which you sit in a metal seat with your feet lying flat on the floor. Because I'm only 5' 1", my feet couldn't reach the floor when I was sitting properly in the chair. (Ah, the perks of my Italian heritage!)

The polygraph examiner, whom I irreverently called Sparkie, quickly remedied the situation by providing me with a wooden box for my feet to rest on. He attached clips to several of my fingers. To my immediate left sat a boxy olive green machine with a long black dial.

Before the test began, Sparkie ordered me to answer with only a *yes* or *no*. The questions began, fired off quickly and to the point. It would be an understatement to say I was nervous -- not because I would lie but because I was hoping the machine wouldn't think I was deceptive. All of this was new to me; I was only 21 years old and had never experienced anything like this before. I was determined to pass this test, so I steadied my heart and nerves as best as I could.

The questions went on for 30 minutes that felt like 30 hours. I was tired and drained by this point, but I didn't let that affect me. I answered every question clearly, concisely, and with complete honesty.

"Have you ever used illegal drugs?"

"No."

He asked me again:

104

"Have you ever used illegal drugs?"

"No."

He asked the question for a third time in a row. "Have you ever used illegal drugs?" I was starting to panic. He had not repeated any of the other previous questions. Was the machine registering something? Were its indicators pointing to "liar"?

"NO!"

I had replied more emphatically than I meant to.

"Are you telling the truth?" He asked calmly, his voice never waving.

"Yes. My friends did, but I didn't."

"Please only respond with *yes* or *no*. Have you ever used illegal drugs?"

"No," I repeated for the fourth time, holding back from defending myself any more.

I was telling the truth, and my heart sank thinking he might not believe me or that the machine was telling him otherwise. How is this possible? This couldn't be how I end up: failing this polygraph and losing the opportunity to work in law enforcement.

Finally, Sparkie spoke again.

"Sorry about that. It is part of the test, to see how well you handle being under pressure. I have no doubt you have told nothing but the truth. Good job!"

Thank goodness. I never knew my deodorant could fail me so many times in one day.

Once I had completed the test, Sparkie excused me, informing me that someone from the sheriff's department would be in touch soon with their final decision. Leaving the building, I felt as if I had aged ten years. Polygraph testing was intimidating.

Several weeks passed. Finally, I received a phone call from the Sheriff's Department indicating that I had made it to the next round in the application process, for which I would be required to attend the Law Enforcement Academy. The commitment entailed 450 hours of unpaid classroom training, held in the Patrol Division's office two nights weekly and one entire weekend day. Having made the cut, I could now rest more easily, although I still had to face the rigors of the Academy.

The Academy's regimen consisted of learning and understanding the law, gaining firearm proficiency, and mastering field training. Having aced a BB gun earlier in life, I was confident that the range targets would be easier to hit than tin cans.

I was sure that this was going to be a walk in the park.

THE BB GUN

The Academy brought new meaning to the word *stress* – especially on the firing line. Target shooting brought me back to my anxious youthful efforts to persuade my parents to let me have a BB gun.

Our parents had purchased a cabin near the town of Forestville – sixty-five miles north of San Francisco near the Russian River – nestled in a wooded area rich with the aroma of country living. The cabin's appeal made me feel as if I were in heaven. Made of real wood siding, the cabin featured a covered front porch, two bedrooms, a fireplace, a small kitchen and an unfinished side area.

The previous owners had constructed the house a few years earlier as a getaway from the hustle and bustle of city life. Russian River was a unique area, dotted with summer homes for those living in the Bay Area. This cozy atmosphere allowed the residents to step away from a busy life and enjoy downtime in this quiet, quaint community.

Traveling to the cabin presented a challenge in the form of a steep uphill climb on an extremely narrow, twisting road. But it was well worth the journey. At the top, where the road leveled off, the view was breathtaking.

Whenever we arrived at the cabin, I wasted no time embarking on my woodsy adventures, on which I invariably encountered a wild creature or two. (Even a few bats paid me a visit). It wasn't long before I realized I might need a little-added protection from strangers or wild animals. After considering my options, I ask my parents for permission to buy a BB gun

(This was taking place at a time when it was normal for kids, specifically boys, to own a BB gun – if not more potent weapons.)

One afternoon, shopping at the Payless Drug Store with my mom, I noticed a Daisy BB Gun, #102 Model 36. It was nickel plated, featuring a wood stock, pump action, and a capacity of 500 BBs – which reduced reloading time. I could see that it was easy to operate.

"Sir, is it possible to check out that Daisy BB Gun? I would like to see if it fits me, "I asked the store clerk.

"Is this for you, little lady?"

"Yes."

For some unknown reason, he laughed and refused to allow me a chance to examine the gun.

"These guns are for boys, not girls."

Undeterred, I asked, "I know. May I see it please?"

At that time my mother showed up inquiring what I was "up to." *Up to* – I never felt I was up to anything; so why did my mother always think I was up to something?

"Checking out a BB Gun."

108

By that squinty-eyed look on my mother's face – the one she wore when the answer was NO – I could tell she was not at all amused.

I was not going to give up so easily. I began to plead with her, "Please mom, pretty, pretty, please! I promise I will take good care of it and be extra safe. I won't ever misuse it or let anyone else shoot it. Please!" We stood there looking at each other inconclusively as I put on my best puppy-dog face.

At this point the sales clerk chuckled. "I tried to tell her, Ma'am, that BB guns are for boys only, not toys for little girls."

My mother let out a resigned sigh, straightened her shoulders, and turned to the sales clerk.

"Well, I guess today is an exception. I will take one of those BB guns for my daughter, please."

The clerk's jaw practically hit the floor.

What? I thought. I couldn't believe it! My mother was going to buy me a BB gun! My heart almost jumped out of my chest. In our constant butting of heads, had I finally achieved a victory?

I didn't know why she agreed to buy the gun, but I wasn't going to ask lest she change her mind.

"Don't make me regret this decision, Teresa."

"I promise I won't!"

Once the transaction was complete, I grabbed the BB gun box, tucked it under my arm, and skipped all the way out of the store to the car, happy as a mosquito in a nudist colony.

The next morning, I gathered up as many old tin cans and makeshift targets as I could for my first practice session. If I was going to carry this BB gun around, I'd better learn how to use it. I placed my targets so as not to be shooting towards the adjoining property. It would not be propitious for my continued possession of the gun were I to take out a neighbor or two.

I lined up the cans, spreading them out to give the cans room to travel once I hit them. After I loaded the BBs through the end of the barrel, checked the gun, and gave it a pump, the gun was ready. Having learned from books and TV that I needed to sight up my target, I looked through the front sight, lined it up with the rear sight, and, holding steady, pulled the trigger.

"BANG."

From the looks of the target, I was clearly no threat to Annie Oakley. I whispered to myself, "This will take practice."

I must have gone through a hundred BBs before I hit my first can. It was a good thing we did not have a metal detector; with all the BBs lying around, the thing would be screaming. Eager to gain experience with my BB gun, I practiced until my trigger finger hurt. Before long, I was hitting each can every time. "Ping! Ping! Ping!" What a beautiful sound!

I was ready.

One Friday evening in Richmond we headed to the cabin in the woods. The next morning, I rose early, prepared a few snacks, grabbed my gun, wrapped up a lunch in a red handkerchief, tied it around the gun, placed the gun on my shoulder, and headed off into the woods.

Owning a gun takes considerable responsibility and common sense. To that end, my father had taught me to never aim my gun at anything I didn't want to kill. The gun was for my protection from wild animals during my discoveries of the wooded area around the cabin – not for pleasure killing. I loved animals, and the thought of killing one never crossed my mind, either, unless one was about to have me for lunch. I promised my parents I would never point or shoot the gun needlessly. During the entire remainder of the summer I observed that rule.

I was soon to learn that the definition of *needlessly* might be a matter of opinion . . .

A Halloween to Remember

Two months later, as Halloween approached in Richmond, my parents promised my youngest brother Donny, age five, that they would take him trick-or-treating. Unfortunately, they found themselves otherwise occupied and therefore unable to fulfill their promise. After I returned from trick-or-treating myself, my mother asked me if I would be a good sister and go trick-or-treating with Donny, who had been in his skeleton costume since dinnertime.

I agreed to escort Donny through our neighborhood, where there had been considerable turmoil from the recent riots. To protect Donny's candy, I took along my BB gun. We were quite a pair: a young would- be Annie Oakley packing a gun to protect a walking skeleton.

I had never been afraid of guns; I enjoyed playing cops and robbers, always taking the role of the cop. So carrying the gun as a precaution felt natural to me.

Donny, smiling broadly, pillowcase in hand for capturing the candy, happily headed out the door under my protection. It was a cool October night and most of the neighborhood kids had already made their rounds.

Knocking on doors, going from house to house, Donny was beaming from ear to ear, his pillowcase filling up with all kinds of goodies, which he kept checking. I persuaded him to wait until we were back home before taking inventory.

Our journey was nearly completed when we encountered a house that presented quite a tall staircase leading to the front door. Having stopped for a moment and contemplated whether to make the climb, we then undertook the effort, working hard to reach the top. Our petite bodies and short legs made the trip a challenge.

Looking up at what seemed to be an endless procession of steps, we stopped half way to catch our breath. Gazing up at those stairs seemed like looking up at a skyscraper. Finally at the top, Donny knocked on the door; we waited with bated breath. No one answered. He knocked again; still no answer.

"Donny let's go. No one is home."

Turning to head down the long flight of stairs, I noticed, at the bottom, two dangerous looking juveniles staring up at us – and yelling that when we got down there, they were going to kick our butts and steal Donny's candy.

Hearing this, Donny broke out in tears, hiding behind me, pleading, "Please don't let them steal my candy. Please!" This confrontation appeared to be a standoff until the juveniles started up the stairs.

In a split second, my protective instincts kicked in and, I raised my BB gun, shouting, "If you come up the stairs, I'll shoot."

The name-calling intensified as they started toward the first step,

"Just you wait till we get you."

Giving the gun a pump, I took aim and fired, hitting one of the villains in the shoulder. I couldn't pump that gun fast enough; they kept advancing, the shooting continued, every round hitting them until they retreated.

I knew the 500-round capacities would come in handy!

"You better run, or I'll keep shooting."

Don looked up at me, his tears quickly drying,

113

"Are they gone?"

"Yes."

This was our opportunity to run and escape this ordeal. Don placed a secure hold on his pillowcase of candy; while I held his hand.

"Run!"

It took us far less time to travel down the steps than it did to go up. Once at the bottom, we ran like scalded apes, looking back to ensure the offenders were not after us.

We flew through the neighborhood towards our house, barely checking for traffic, in a dead run. After jumping up our front steps and flinging the front door open, Donny and I stood there, out of breath, trying to regain our composure.

Mom was there as we entered.

"What is wrong with you two? You look like you have seen a ghost?"

Huffing and puffing I replied, "Well, not a ghost, just two bullies who were trying to ruin my little brother's Halloween."

Looking concerned my mother asked, "Are you two all right?"

After I had a chance to explain to my mom what had occurred she said, "I'm proud of you Teresa; you protected both your brother and yourself. You really are good with that BB gun."

I beamed at her praise. As crazy as the night had been, my silver lining was my mother's glimpse of the real me. Not the daughter she tried to turn into a "lady"– but the daughter who protected her brother by responsibly using a gun, something only boys were supposed to do.

I have a feeling my brother and I won't be the only ones remembering that Halloween. In fact, many years later, I myself was remembering that dramatic incident while I waited at the Sheriff's Department firing range in order to qualify as a Deputy.

***

This first day at the shooting range, I needed to complete the Academy's requirements. Still inexperienced with a handgun, I was excited, eager, and nervous all in the same moment. My weapon of choice was a borrowed six-inch Smith and Wesson 357 revolver. (As a Reserve Deputy, we were required to supply all of our own equipment, including a $50.00 badge deposit.)

Breathing hard and listening to the Range Master's every command, I was instructed to begin qualifying. It was imperative to pass this portion of the academy. If I failed, I failed the Academy, disqualifying me as a Deputy.

Shooting my BB gun had given me confidence as a shooter, but this was different. I was shooting at targets from various angles and distances in a limited time. Although my BB gun had presented no recoil, this 357 revolver kicked like a mule.

Demonstrating quick-reloading skills, taking cover, and thinking on my feet presented challenges I had not yet experienced; but here I was. The range was located miles out of town. Very little asphalt covered the area, and performing my maneuvers on dirt was definitely a challenge. But in a real life situation, I could not pick and choose the terrain.

As we lined up at the 25 yard line, the Range Master yelled, "Range is hot. On the command, begin shooting."

Giving the class specific instructions on how many rounds to shoot, and where to place them on the target before re-holstering, the Range Master commanded, "Gun!"

My heart almost popped out of my chest. I grabbed my revolver, pushing it quickly forward out of the holster and, setting my sights, began firing.

At first the intense recoil was a surprise. Realizing I needed a stronger grip, I gave the gun more control. Although my first rounds were not spot on, they were still within the targeted area. Completing the twenty 25 yard line, I moved to the 15, then the 7, each time gaining confidence. But, from the looks of my target, I still needed a lot of improvement.

The Range Master patiently coached me in order to calm me down and help me stay focused – causing me even further excitement and nervousness in anticipation of finally passing.

The day seemed endless as our group of rookies kept shooting until all of us qualified. It took me two times to pass, not because I couldn't shoot; my problem was that my anticipation of the gun's recoil was causing me to miss my target. But that was a problem I overcame, (as I would many other problems in the future.) And my joy in qualifying at the shooting range brought me a chuckle at the irony:

One long-ago Halloween, I protected my little brother; now I would be protecting my fellow citizens.

GOING UNDER COVER

Standing proud behind the badge had been my lifelong dream. Those wishing to barricade my progress discovered their efforts were thwarted by the fire burning within me, powering me towards my dreams – a fire raging like a volcano making ready to erupt.

Growing up watching "Charlie's Angels" and "Police Woman", I always dreamed of getting a taste of the undercover life – wired for sound, dressed up and portraying a character far different from my usual persona.

Law enforcement is not your average, nine-to-five career, at least not for me. As the youngest female on the force, willing to engage in all aspects of police work, I jumped at opportunities whenever they arose.

Early one wintry morning, I received a phone call from the Sergeant of Detectives, Mark Howell, who asked me to stop by his office for a quick chat. Later that afternoon, after completing my shift at my regular job as a mechanic, I headed to the Sheriff's Department at around 4 PM.

Sgt. Howell sat waiting at his desk.

"Hi, Sergeant. What's up?"

"Well, Teresa, we have a special assignment coming up that is somewhat dangerous for which we need a young female to play the role of a prostitute. Since you are the youngest female we have and the other Deputies have shown great respect for your performance, I wanted to inquire if you were up to the task."

"I see, Sergeant. Can you tell me more."

Sgt. Howell took a deep breath.

"The assignment will require you to go undercover on a drug bust. In order to infiltrate this drug ring, we need two deputies, one male and one female, to fill the roles of drug buyers. You would be teamed up with Sgt. Mike Wallace, who is currently working undercover on the case. We will be scheduling a meeting to pass off the drugs. Once we have confirmation of the meeting, we'll know the time and location. Sgt. Wallace will make the contact. He will portray your pimp. Once the deal goes down, you will stay in character."

"Not like I could do much else rigged up like a prostitute. Will I be wired and armed?"

"Yes, on both counts, plus you will need to dress the part, complete with wig and short skirt, high heels, and heavy makeup that matches your character. How does that sound? Are you up for the challenge?"

"Wow, this is something I have never done before, but I am willing to give it my all if you need me."

"Great. Once I have more information, I will get back to you on this. Please keep this to yourself, for the protection of all involved."

I left the Sergeant's office, my eyes wide, completely puzzled wondering what I just gotten myself into. If this were not done correctly, it could go awfully wrong. What if the wireless microphones failed or my

118

cover was detected? (Now, that was an alarming thought!) I kept trying to convincing myself that I could do this. One comforting thought was that there would be plainclothes deputies nearby.

Going under cover was never addressed in Police Academy 101. This assignment, as intense as it was, frightened me in many ways. Could this tomboy pull it off? The clothes, the hair – oh no, the hair! I would need Aqua Net, the very substance I despised!

It was time to prepare, so I contacted my girlfriend Nancy Johnson for assistance. Unable to confess my reasoning for dressing up as a prostitute, I nevertheless sensed she was aware as to why. Getting sized for my character clothing was comical as I donned a wig and fishnet nylons. I was beginning to realize that this was not a TV show or a novel; this was the real thing – with no time to turn back. The contacts had been made, the time, and everyone in place. Never having been a "girl's girl", I asked myself, *Can I really do this?*

On my way to meet Sgt. Wallace, I placed about three sticks of gum in my mouth, not just for appearance but to help calm my nerves. Sgt. Wallace was an ace; with several years'experience as a detective, he was a polished professional. I, on the other hand, was a rookie at this sort of thing. One wrong move – or one wrong word-could get us into cement overshoes.

We were to meet the drug dealers near downtown Reno at a quaint little Mexican restaurant promptly at 5 p.m. Going over a few last-minute details, my heart was racing and so was my gum-chewing. My skirt squeezed me like a king cobra. I kept wondering how the heck women wear these things. And those lethal stiletto shoes. . .

When we arrived, Sgt. Wallace yanked me out of the car to show that he was in control. (If he had known how hard it was to walk in those shoes, he may have been a bit less aggressive.) Entering the restaurant, we were approached by two large males, the first a bag of bones, sporting thinning hair, rotten teeth, a thin build, and baggy pants. The second looked as if he belonged in a biker bar, with a six-foot build, greasy brown hair, scraggly beard, and tattoos out of a horror movie. Without a doubt, they were armed; drug dealing and artillery go hand in hand.

Both appeared to be nervous and anxious at the same time. They quickly sat us down at a table close to the door. I scanned the room for our plainclothes deputies and for anyone that might be suspicious. My eye noticed one of our backups at the bar and another one eating alone. My "pimp" sat adjacent to me, as I remained tethered by fear. I sat patiently while the boys discussed the deal – loud enough, luckily, to be picked up by my wire.

I knew that part of my role that evening was to be a distraction, eye candy for the men. I could see that it was working, because Biker Dude was clearly hot about the cut of my jib. I cringed as I caught him staring at me with a creepy grin.

He turned to Sgt. Wallace.

"So, is this one for sale?"

Sgt. Wallace stroked my arm.

"She is a pretty one, isn't she? Let's consider her your treat after this deal goes down."

Biker Dude's grin grew wider.

The thought of becoming his property made me choke, causing me to almost swallow my gum. However, I was relieved to know this creep had thoroughly bought into my character – which was critical considering that these dirtbags were in the process of sizing us up before allowing us to meet with the ringleader.

Apparently we passed muster, because these thugs immediately escorted us out to the parking lot. Suddenly Bag of Bones grabbed us, demanding that we ride with them if we wanted this deal. I avoided eye contact with Sgt. Wallace, which would have betrayed our fear. Accommodating our captors, we entered the rear door of their menacing black sedan.

Too bad I didn't own a stop watch; my racing heart may have set a world record.

Our destination, the MGM Grand Hotel, was not far from the restaurant, and I hoped our undercover peeps were hot on our tail. One wrong move and we would be roommates with Jimmy Hoffa.

During the short jaunt, Sgt. Wallace and the drug dealers made small talk while I maintained the silence befitting anyone struggling with a mini skirt to keep from exposing herself. But this was not a time to be shy. I chomped harder on my gum, keeping my eyes peeled for our backup.

121

The two-mile drive felt like two hours, but we finally arrived unharmed at the entrance to the casino. Bag of Bones parked the car closest to the front doors. Sgt. Wallace let me exit first; I glanced around quickly but not so noticeably as to suggest I was looking for someone.

As we entered the casino, I was instantly alarmed to recognize my friend Jamie Shaheen playing the piano just inside the entrance. My heart hit the floor. If Jamie acknowledged that she knew me, or started asking questions out loud, this could get ugly. I would not make eye contact with her. I hoped that she would know that this getup was out of character for me; I prayed she would understand that I was on duty.

As we approached, I noticed a solitary, heavy set, Italian-looking male whose eyes intensely locked on us. By the menacing look on his face, I could see that he was the ringleader.

We all sat down in an area concealed from other patrons, where the ringleader began the conversation, wanting to know if we had brought the money for the buy. Sgt. Wallace presented a bag from his coat pocket, not wanting to hand it over until the drugs were observed.

At that point, the ringleader presented a bag of his own, giving it to Sgt. Wallace to examine. The officer looked it over closely to make sure it was what they had agreed upon. Then he nodded, the signal for our backups to move in and for me to hit the floor.

At that point, as the ringleader reached for the envelope, Sgt. Wallace clutched the ringleader's arm and slammed him into the chair. The takedown happened so fast that, the next thing I knew, I had been thrown to the floor by one of the undercover deputies, while the others disarmed and handcuffed Bag of Bones and Biker Dude.

My short skirt nearly baring it all as I lay on the floor, I was glad the lights were dim. Once the scene was secured, it was safe to rise. As graceful as one can be in stilettos and a miniskirt as tight as a bullet proof vest, I managed to stand up. The takedown had been carefully crafted, the apprehension assigned to the undercover peeps instead of to me. (It would have been very difficult to wrestle anyone in that microscopic skirt and those insane shoes!)

Startled by the violent takedown, Jamie, the piano player, unwittingly up-tempoed her ballad to the pace of a rock song. She clearly had no idea of what had just happened, nor could I stay and chat with her about it.

We arrested all three, charging them with trafficking of a controlled substance. Carefully stiletto-prancing out to the parking area with all the other "fully clothed" deputies, I noticed open-mouthed patrons staring at me – no doubt assuming by my attire that I was among this unsavory crew that had been so deservedly busted.

Taking stock of this assignment, I found myself reflecting back to the beginning of my law enforcement career and how far I had come. It seemed only a moment in time since the doubting Mrs. Wheeler had disparaged my potentialities as an effective police officer.

If only she could have seen me now. . .

DEATH OF A KING

I came to understand early on that one must do what is right, not what is easy. But, fighting for equality and pursing my dreams was never a war I envisioned on enlisting in. Society's campaign against women entering a so-called *Man's World* declared war on any female who crossed that threshold: just as Mr. Pallozari did when forced to allow me, his female student, to cross the entrance into his classroom. Negroes were also pushing the envelope and fighting for equality – something I shared without realizing it.

Leaving Elementary School and advancing to Adams Junior High for my 7th and 8th grades failed to offer the freedom I had been searching for. Girls wore only skirts with blouses, or dresses, as our daily attire. I was never comfortable donning these types of clothes. I felt as if I was wearing a Halloween costume. I envied the boys for being allowed to wear pants while girls had to be prim and proper, showing off their place in society by dressing in the most feminine style available.

One spring day there came a major breakthrough: a local law allowing girls to wear pants to school. My mother knew this would be the end to her constant persistence in trying to make me into a lady. From that moment on, all the skirts and blouses I owned would remain forever abandoned in my closet. I was now permitted to wear the clothes that represented me: short sleeve t-shirts and pants, not girly clothes dictated by my mother or society.

Going to school in pants was a liberty I proudly displayed. This gave me independence to engage in other types of activities, like being a Hall Monitor;

something out of reach while I was attired in a skirt. The school halls were orderly thanks to the presence of hall monitors. Students who applied were chosen by grade average and good attendance for this position.

The school utilized students to help maintain order on the school grounds before, during and after school. Still dreaming of one day standing behind a badge and defending law and order, I learned of an opening for a Hall Monitor, for which I eagerly applied, waiting patiently after submitting my application.

If students were caught running in the halls, throwing trash on the floor without picking it up, smoking in the bathroom, or failing to correct their previous warnings, a Hall Monitor issued a citation.

There was ranking among the Hall Monitors, all the way to Lieutenant. I wanted to be a part of this elite group – not because I wished to be the strong arm of the school halls, but because I believed in law and order.

Having shortly received a notice of acceptance as a Hall Monitor from the principal, I was excited to be offered this position, and, in no time, I moved up to the rank of Lieutenant. Unfortunately, that position brought me occasional unpleasant moments of giving my closest friends citations and several warnings. (Anytime you represent the law, your list of friends tends to shrink.)

With the rank of Lieutenant came responsibilities. I didn't take my position as Hall monitor lightly. I was there to ensure the students remained safe and obeyed the school rules. As the Lieutenant, my duties were to arrive at school early and shelter the front door, admitting teachers as they arrived and keeping students out until the first bell rang, indicating they could enter.

One April morning, I arrived at school early as usual. But this was not just any ordinary day; it was the day after a king was murdered – that is, Dr. Martin Luther King, Jr., a renowned leader for equality and a voice for African Americans. Dr. King was a social activist and Baptist minister who played a key role in the American civil rights movement from the mid-1950s until his assassination on April 4, 1968.

Dr. King sought equality and human rights for African Americans, the economically disadvantaged, and all victims of injustice, through peaceful protest. He was the driving force behind watershed events such as the Montgomery Bus Boycott and the 1963 March on Washington, which helped bring about such landmark legislation as the Civil Rights Act 1964 and the Voting Rights Act 1965.

On that fateful morning after Dr. King's assassination, I stood at the front doors observing students as they were dropped off by their parents in the traffic circle in front of the school. The students gathered, waiting for the bell to ring and for me to open the doors.

Pacing back and forth behind the front doors, I heard a commotion out front near the circle area. I looked out the doors to see what was happening. At first, I could not comprehend what was actually taking place. Students began running in all directions, and I saw African-Americans throwing rocks at Caucasians walking or driving into the area.

Trying to decipher the situation, I observed students running towards the front doors, right where I was standing, pounding on the glass to enter. They kept gesturing at me to unlock the doors and allow them in for safety. However, my instructions were to not unlock the doors until the bell rang. I was at a crossroads. My mind kept saying *unlock the door,* but my duty side was yelling back, *no, that would violate my orders.*

Suddenly, the doors to the front office flew open to reveal the principal running out, yelling, "Do not open the front doors! The police are on their way."

I was horrified, torn between helping my schoolmates or carrying out my orders. This was more than I could stand; after a few minutes observing this horrific ordeal, I decided to escape by running to the girls' restroom, leaving the principal to deal with it all.

As I sat in the restroom trying to regain my composure and comprehend why this was happening, I could hear screaming coming from the halls echoing from the outside. Not ready to stick my neck out just yet, I stood there trembling in hopes that the horror underway outside would not enter my safe space.

At that point, I heard Police sirens. In response, the sounds of students screaming seemed to diminish a bit. I decided to give a peek into the hallway, opening the bathroom door just enough to see if it was safe to leave my cover. Teachers were running upstairs and trying to figure out what to do.

The teachers were there to protect us, but this day suggested otherwise. For me to have opened the doors would have been a disaster, with people running for cover and protesters in pursuit of them. The students weren't the ones creating the mayhem; their attackers were teenagers and adults waging war over the killing of their King.

Soon the police moved in, taking control of the school. The principal canceled school, simply requesting parents to retrieve their children. Some students were sent to local hospitals for treatment, while many of the protesters were arrested.

I couldn't understand why some many people saw violence as the main choice of change, when the non-violent nature of Dr. King's mission was clear. He had been peacefully fighting for equality among all races, a fight which ended his life – but not his legacy.

I have a dream – a common ground that Dr. King and I shared. He was dreaming of equal rights, while I was dreaming of acceptance.

POLICE ASSISTANCE LEAGUE DRILL TEAM
Petaluma Ladies Placed First

Marching, Boys, and Wooden Rifles

Martin Luther King had lost his life pursing a dream, paradoxically pursued after his death in the form of rioting by his followers – dissidents marching for equality. These dissidents and I had something in common: I was struggling for equality as well, marching on the road to fulfillment of my dreams – most notably in the shape of a balanced and fair work environment.

My life in Petaluma was taking form. I was settling in nicely, and my desire to do more with my life was growing stronger. However, for a considerable period of time, I was uncertain as how to make that desire a reality. Fortunately, at that time a high school friend offered me a friendly suggestion about auditions underway for applicants to the Police Assistant League (PAL) Drill Team (all girls), sponsored by the local Police Department.

PAL was recruiting girls aged twelve to eighteen. Being seventeen, I fit perfectly within the age group they were looking for. This appealed to me, so I went by the Police station and picked up an application from an officer who indicated that tryouts would begin the following weekend.

Arriving at the tryouts, I quickly realized by my tomboyish appearance that I was not like any of the other girls. However, I wasn't deterred, even though I had big doubts that I would even make the cut. (I had never been one to worry about my looks; I had always been content in my own skin. Instead, it was others who often judged me for my tomboyish style, and I knew from experience that society prefers pretty, feminine women.

At a height of 5'1" and weighing no more than a buck-o-one, I was not only a tomboy but a small one to boot.)

As I waited for the tryouts to begin, I scanned around the room. There must have been over thirty girls waiting to try out, some of the girls grouped together, others practicing their marching, and still others doing stretching exercises. Since this was my first time marching, I was unsure how to prepare. I paid close attention to the girls practicing. I watched their movements as they turned right, then left, and then about-face.

Ken, the drill team coordinator, placed us in groups of nine, instructing everyone about what he was looking for in the team members and about what we were to perform when commanded by the team leader. At this point, I was turned over to my team leader, Michelle Dawson. Dark haired, small framed, her back ramrod-straight, her head lofty above her shoulders, she walked like an elegant race horse, prancing as she commanded us. Before we were to stage in front of the evaluators, Michelle went over a few basic commands. I found myself easily following along. I, too, was confident I could accomplish this drill; I was determined to conquer this audition.

Once Michelle felt that we had adequately practiced, we were formed into three parallel lines facing the drill team board, comprised of the drill team commander, a lieutenant, and a police officer from the Petaluma Police Department. They were to evaluate how well we stayed in formation, how well we executed our turns, how well our arms moved, and how dedicated we were to our efforts.

Michelle, standing in front of us, gave us a quick nod, indicating we were about to begin.

"Forward March!" she commanded. "Left face! Right face!"

Having marched for several minutes, I felt at times as if my legs would collapse beneath me. But I kept going. Marching and turning, consumed with fatigue, I fell in love with it all with every step I took. Working as a team was exhilarating. I knew I had to be a part of this.

The tryouts, two hours of intense maneuvers, felt good. Exhausted, my legs feeling like Jell-O, I was excused. Ken called the teams over, informing us that we would be notified within the next few days as to whether we had made the cut.

Three excited days passed before I received the call; it was the Police lieutenant notifying me that I had been accepted as a PAL drill team member. He was firm in describing the major commitment required by the team as well as the many hours expected. Practice sessions were to be held after school and on weekends, three hours a day. I made it clear to him that I was equal to the challenge.

"Ok, then I will see you Saturday for your first practice."

I waited until he hung up before I screamed.

"Thank you, God." I knew I was up for this demanding commitment.

Practice began immediately. The workout was intense; this was not a time to be out of shape. Ken had us exercise first to limber up and then mark time standing against the wall for thirty grueling minutes -- knees raised to a uniform height, backs straight, eyes forward.

Then we practiced saluting until we all had it right. We learned maneuvers: right and left turns, marching, staying in step, all lines straight. As we marched, our arms had to swing in perfect parallel. The drill proceeded until we looked as if we were one. The practicing was truly paying off, and I had become addicted to the precision. Likewise, it wasn't long before the team had become a marching machine.

After several weeks of intense practicing, we were told that our first performance would take place in a few weeks, during a parade honoring the return home of a local Vietnam soldier. This invitation was a great honor, and I knew we were ready. I could feel it in my bones.

Finally, the day of the parade arrived. As we alighted from the bus, Michelle gathered us near the staging area for a pep talk.

"Okay, girls, you have been practicing for months. Just listen to my commands, remember to work off each other, and we will march away looking like pros. Let's show off all your hard work."

Lining up in the middle of the street, nervous, anxious and scared all at the same time, we couldn't let down our local soldier or our team leader, Michelle. Nerves and all, I knew we could do this. We were ready.
The command came.

"Line up!" Michelle barked. "Attention, forward march!"

My heart pounding, I began to sweat as we began marching. I kept my peripheral vision locked onto the girl to my left. Concentrating on my spot in the last row on the right end, making sure my footsteps and hand movements were even with those on my left, I listened to every command Michelle yelled out."Left, left, left-right-left." Michelle turned at times to insure we were all still present and looking sharp.

We marched toward the center of the parade where our grand performance was to take place for the spectators and judges. At this point, I began to worry. *Would I remember my counts for the formation we practiced?* If I messed up and missed my mark in the formation, the rest of us would be thrown off.

As we arrived at the grandstand area and Michelle had given the command "Move!" we began our maneuvers, executing our turns, each of us staying in step and holding our own. From my viewpoint, we were spectacular. I could feel an electric excitement not only within me but in the air as well. My stomach in knots, sweat rolling down my brow, my body feeling numb, I nevertheless felt euphoric.

The last maneuver complete, Michelle brought us back to our formation, marching us to the finish line and dismissing us. We immediately began to huddle around Ken, who was beaming from ear to ear.

"You ladies were fantastic! Great job! The crowd was more than impressed, and I am so proud of you all."

It all felt so good inside; I couldn't wait for the next time. Proud parents and families of the other girls had seen and been amazed by our performance. As for me – my father working seven days a week and my mother tending to two younger brothers – I had to be my own cheering section. (Even though we were a tight-knit family, the absence of a parent at a major passage had never upset me before and wasn't bothering me now. I wasn't seeking approval as much as progress toward my dreams.)

***

One evening during my drill-team days, after cruising the Boulevard in my parents' Cadillac, I stopped by Denny's to hang out with my girl friends. The restaurant was jam packed with many cruisers. Since the place was so full, we tried cramming as many of our group into a booth as we could.

Sitting in the booth next to us was an older boy, Ron Nelson, who had graduated the year prior and was now working at the local Lucky grocery store.

Ron was a tall, soft spoken youth whose arresting blue eyes were amply set off by his collar-length blond hair. Although he had graduated from Petaluma High, our paths had never crossed in school. I found him attractive, but – not particularly interested in boys – I didn't pay him much attention.

While we girls were sipping our milk shakes and laughing over something stupid, I glanced over at the table where Ron was seated, his attention focused on us. Rising from his seat, he walked over to our table, staring at me. I thought, *He can't be looking at me? He must be interested in one of the beauties sitting next to me at the table.*

"Can I join you ladies?" he politely inquired.

We laughed like silly schoolgirls, the six of us crammed in so tightly that we couldn't even raise an arm.

Ron, with his sapphire blue eyes beaming my direction, asked me, "Would you like to join me at my table?"

At first I looked around to see if maybe he was speaking to one of the other girls.

"Are you asking *me* to join you?" I asked, pointing to myself.

"Yes, you. What's your name?"

"T-Teresa," I stuttered.

He extended his right hand to me, my jaw dropping slightly in shock.

It took me a second to regain my composure. After sitting motionless for a moment like a deer in the headlights, I asked the girls to let me out. Still in shock, I joined Ron at his table.

The ensuing conversation was idle chit-chat: the usual exchange of information about favorite activities and plans for the future. I was feeling very uncomfortable. I didn't know what to say to Ron. It all felt like a dream, not reality. Soon it was time to go, and we both said our polite goodbyes after exchanging phone numbers.

After Ron had left, I returned to sit with my girlfriends. We giggled about my sitting with a boy, and then a flood of questions began. Not enthusiastic about dating, I confessed that we had exchanged phone numbers – indicating that, as far as I was concerned, if Ron were to call, that would be fine; if not, that would be fine, too.

One of the girls, Janice, declared, "Well, if you pass him up, send him my way."

After a few days had passed, I found myself at Lucky's picking out apples. Surprised, I looked up to see Ron standing there with a smirk on his face. At first I thought this encounter might have been happenstance; but, after observing Ron's apron, I realized that he worked in the produce section.

"Hi, Teresa. Good to see you again."

"Hi, Ron. Nice to see you too."

After a few moments of exchanged pleasantries and small talk, Ron asked, "If you're not doing anything this Friday night, would you like to have dinner with me?"

Frozen in place, unsure of what to say, I didn't know if I was excited or comatose. But I thought *what the heck?*

"OK, Ron. That sounds nice."

Walking out of the store afterward, I considered that this was would be my first date since David. Was I ready for a relationship with another boy? I was still feeling raw over David's death. I had dreams, and boys would just get in the way of them. I had known early on that marriage was not for me; I had things to accomplish, and I was going to make them happen.

Ron owned his own car, a Ford four-door, jacked up in the back with mag wheels and sporting the newest style 8-track tape player with an impressive selection of artists. This seemed ideal to me, because I love music.

This first date was bringing back some strong emotions about David, the first boy I really liked, only to lose tragically. That loss had caused me some major insecurities about life and how quickly it can end.

As we began to drive off to dinner, Ron asked what type of music I liked and asked me to pick one of the 8-track tapes in his collection. I noticed one that appeared to have been a mix of songs he had recorded himself, labeled *Various Hits*. I chose that one and inserted it into the player located under the dash. Immediately, the first song began to play.

I froze in my seat. I didn't know what to say or even what to feel. The very first song playing on this tape was *Last Kiss*, the very song that David and I had considered "ours" – the same song that David had told me represented him watching over me. This was getting weird. I looked around as if someone else might be in the car with us. How could this be? Was David watching out for me? Was it a sign from David to let me know everything was OK? I almost stopped breathing. I could still hear David's voice describing *Last Kiss*.

Ron could sense that something was amiss.

139

"Teresa, is that song upsetting you?"

"No, Ron, nothing is wrong. I just think of an old friend whenever I hear that song."

After dinner, Ron removed the tape, turned to me, and, reaching out with the tape in his hand, said, "Since *Last Kiss* means so much to you, I want you to have this tape."

I slowly reached for the tape with my right hand, thinking, *OK, David, you will forever be in my corner. Thanks for sharing the evening with me.*

I knew it was time to let him go.

Thereafter, my relationship with Ron was respectful and genuine, but I was not in love. I still wasn't sure what love is. Ron never tried to force himself on me; he was the true meaning of a nice guy – kind, unselfish, and generous. For example, he frequently offered me his car when my parents needed the Cadillac. The car had a locking gas cap, to which I never needed the key. Ron always made sure the tank was full when I drove it.

One thing Ron was passionate about was his teeth. He had bright white teeth and worked hard to keep them that way. In his car he kept Pearl White Tooth Drops to help maintain that brightness. Accordingly, my friend Gina Lucas and I ginned up a nickname for him: Pearly White – which never seemed to bother him. He must have known that we intended it as a compliment.

On Valentine's Day that year, 1973, Ron sent me a dozen roses and took me to dinner. It was a quiet evening, just the two of us. As we began our dessert, Ron looked at me, reached in his coat pocket, and pulled out a small gift.

"Teresa, will you marry me?"

In total shock, I didn't know what to say. This was all so sudden. It was hard to even collect my feelings. Ron, placing a stunning sapphire-diamond ring on my finger, asked me to think about his proposal. The ring was beautiful, encompassing – thoughtfully – my birthstone. Still in shock, I was still feeling overwhelmed. My future lay ahead of me, and I still had to find it. Marriage was not part of the Teresa plan. What did I know about being a wife and/or a mother?

Months went by, and I remained silent on the subject of marriage while still wearing the ring. Meanwhile, Ron sweetly showered me with flowers and gifts. But I was uneasy, feeling that I was living a charade. While I knew in my heart that Ron was a fine man, something was missing: for Ron, true romantic love from me; for me, a proper sense of who I wanted to be. I had to find myself before I could give myself to someone else.

Further complicating matters, Ron's mother wasn't fond of me. Ron was her favorite, and she wasn't about to give up her boy, especially not to me. I represented change and the loss of her son, and that did not sit well with her. I was a new breed of woman who frightened her. His dad wasn't keen on me, either.

In spite of the confusion and overwhelming feelings besetting me, I continued to thrive with the drill team, loving every moment I spent with them. Ron, characteristically, stood by in support of me.

By this time, I had been on the team for over two years. In June of that year, I graduated from high school and, because I was now over-age, had to leave the team – a loss that was hard for me to accept. The drill team had been more than a hobby; it was a passion. My very last march, in September, was a sad day indeed.

During the previous summer, my parents had divorced. The breakup was devastating to me, and I was beyond grateful that I had the team to support me in that difficult time. If it hadn't been for my team members' support and the time I put into practicing, the experience of my family being ripped apart would have been unbearable.

To make matters worse, after the divorce, my mother began dating Lloyd Thomas, whom she had met through my father. Without consulting us kids, Lloyd and my mother decided to leave the area and move themselves, my brothers, and me to southern California, where Lloyd had recently acquired a new job with an ice cream company. This news came as a shock.

When Ron heard the news, he quickly made plans to move along with me. I knew Ron loved me, and I was fond of him; but our engagement had occurred too quickly, too soon, and I was not ready for marriage. I knew I had to face the unpleasant task of letting Ron down – as gently as possible. He thought that he had found his soul mate, and maybe he had; but for me, I was still searching, eager to fill my dreams of being a mechanic and a police officer. Marriage would only interfere.

So I broke it off with Ron. I took off the ring and handed it to him. He graciously declined to accept it, telling me that he wanted me to remember our time together and that the sapphire wasn't his best color anyway. Clearly dejected, head lowered, he walked away without looking back.

The sadness I felt in parting with Ron, unfortunately, was more than matched by my distress at being uprooted again. We were to leave for Los Angeles on the day of my last PAL march – a parade that seemed to proceed in slow motion. I didn't want it to end. Marching the last few steps, saluting for the last time, I bade a teary goodbye to my teammates as I climbed into the Cadillac filled with my possessions. As I drove off, tears rolled down my face. I was leaving behind a town that had become home, filled with wonderful friends whom I would never forget. I may have been in Petaluma only for the previous two years, but I felt that I had made a lifetime's worth of memories.

The drill team had been a collaborative effort. Marching with them had given me a sense of inner power. But I hadn't been merely marching with a team; I had begun marching towards my future.

MIKE THE MECHANIC

Leaving behind my friends and my position on the drill team was profoundly upsetting. It was the second time in almost three years that our family had found a new home, transplanting to an area where the population was enormous compared to Petaluma. Adding to my discomfiture, the drive to Van Nuys was long and depressing.

Lloyd was taking over as General Manager of Tropical Ice Cream. The company owned a fleet of trucks that went out into the neighborhoods peddling ice cream, music amplifying from the trucks PA system, in the hopes that kids would come running to purchase their favorite flavor.

I felt as if my life were being ripped out from under me; I had lost the secure family I once knew. My brothers and I were heading to a city we had no desire to live in and leaving behind my hero: my father. Having recently graduated from high school, I didn't understand what my future held.

It was hard to see the light at the end of the tunnel. I felt insecure and lost. I didn't know Lloyd well enough to form an opinion about him, and my brothers seemed afraid of the uncertainty that Lloyd had brought into our lives.

Housing was expensive for a family of four kids and two adults in Van Nuys, California; the only option was renting a cramped apartment where the boys had to share a bedroom. I was not accustomed to such a large city, and making friends wasn't something I was interested in. I deeply felt that living in Van Nuys would be short-lived. Therefore, I did not want to waste time developing a friendship that might be short-term.

Not knowing a soul outside of the family, we hung close to each other, more for our mutual sanity than anything else. This pattern starkly contrasted with our previous habit of spending pleasant time with relatives and hanging out with friends – all now a distant memory.

Out of school – friendless – my only option was to hang out at Lloyd's new job along with the rest of the family. The apartment was too small, and I wasn't used to being alone. At first, I was crushingly bored, but I soon discovered I could be useful. I was hired at Tropical Ice Cream to work in the freezer loading the trucks in the early morning before the day's deliveries. Although I thought at first I would freeze to death, I soon became acclimated.

At work, I soon met the company mechanic, Mike, who immediately put me at ease with his captivating smile and a larger-than-life positive energy. By now I was beginning to feel a little more optimistic about my new circumstances.

Encouraged by Mike's enthusiasm, I developed the habit of watching him work in the shop repairing the trucks. The shop was like a magnet pulling at me, resonating with my fascination for everything mechanical. This seemed a perfect opportunity for me gain some mechanical experience.

In response to my insatiable curiosity, Mike was exceptionally patient with me, especially with all the questions I was asking about auto mechanics. He never appeared to think me a nuisance.

Mike and I would often discuss my future. He was very supportive of my dreams of one day being a mechanic. Watching him work was a spring-tide rush for me, as I found every aspect of auto repair supremely interesting and energizing. My eyes were glued to Mike's every repair, and my questions were endless.

One afternoon, Mike asked me if I wanted to tackle a repair – with his guidance, of course. Did I! He didn't need to ask me twice. My face was glittering like a spectacularly bright star. This was my first chance at hands-on work, to fix something on a vehicle that needed repair or replacement.

Life in Van Nuys was beginning to take shape, at least for me.

My first assignment was replacing a water pump. Although I was a bit jittery at this first attempt, Mike guided me at each turn of the wrench, showing me how to access a multitude of parts crammed into a small space. Thank goodness for the patience that Mike instilled in me, because otherwise, I might have thrown the tools down and run like hell.

My repair job took more time than Mike would have required to finish it, but his kind voice and extreme patience at every step was invaluable. After finishing the installation, we started the truck and checked for leaks – with none to be found. I felt like a winning prize fighter who had just gone 15 rounds.

As the summer passed, my shop time expanded, and so did my experience and confidence with mechanical repair. The practical education was of incalculable value. However, I was beginning to feel dissatisfied with other aspects of my life.

Stranded at the Ice cream plant during downtime hours, when I was free to leave, I was eager to stretch my space and venture out into the city. My roadblock was in not having wheels of my own.

Still, without the expense of car ownership, and spending most of my free time working at Tropical Ice Cream, I was able to save my earnings – giving me the financial ability to begin hunting for a car of my own. So I would often talk cars with Mike while I helped him in the shop.

One day, as Mike arrived for work, he approached me about a car that a friend of his was selling – a 1963 Chevy Impala. The price was well within my budget: $300.00. Mike had no other details about the car but told me I could check it out after work that day if I was interested. I was indeed interested! That day after work, Mike accompanied me to his friend's house, where the backyard was full of cars.

The white 63 Chevy Impala was resting on jack stands near the front of the yard. The car clearly had sustained some damage to the right front fender and upper control arm which the owner was in the process of repairing. I looked the car over, walked around it, and raised the hood to inspect its 327 engine (with Powerglide transmission.) The brake drums had been painted blue, the interior was tuck-and-roll, and the car was remarkably clean. After discussing matters with the Mike, I paid the $300.00. I was beyond excited – which I did my best not to show too much; otherwise, they both may have thought I was a lunatic. However, I could not take the car with me that evening since the previous (!) owner needed to finish the repairs.

Two days passed before I could take possession of the Impala and drive it home. Sitting behind the wheel, I was in ecstasy. Once I had the car back at the Tropical Ice Cream mechanic shop, Mike asked me if I wanted to learn how to paint a car. Performing body work was not something I thought of doing, nor did I have the experience or desire to try. But I was game.

My painting task was ready at hand. The new fender that had been installed on my car did not match the existing white color of the car. Because Mike wanted me to drive this car with pride and in style, we began a nightly project of prepping the car for painting.

Prep work is the key to a flawless paint job. Therefore, we sanded and sanded and sanded. I thought the sanding would never end; but, as Mike explained, a great foundation makes a great final product. A week later, after work, Mike and I painted the car in the shop. I was in awe of how well I did with the painting. It was all because Mike was a terrific teacher and superbly comforting with his soft-spoken manner. Working with Mike was giving me confidence, friendship, and a priceless education.

Soon enough, my family's sojourn in Van Nuys was ending. One evening we learned our fate: we were leaving Southern California for Reno, Nevada. After only three months in Van Nuys, we were again to be uprooted, this time heading to a new life in Nevada. This prospect was dreadfully sad for me because my only real friend in Van Nuys was Mike, and I feared that this move away from him might bring about the end of my dreams of becoming a mechanic.

The one thing I liked most about Mike was his extraordinarily open mind. He never bowed to a desire for social acceptance; he maintained his own standard: to be kind and helpful to anyone that may need a hand. Mike clearly felt safe as his own person. He saw my passion for a dream, and he did whatever he could to help me spread my wings, whereas most would have clipped them and turned away.

Some might have seen Mike as less than masculine; but to me, he was a giant. He extended a hand to me, and I took it. To him, I wasn't just a girl trying to infiltrate a man's world; I was a young woman pursuing a dream, and he wanted to cheer me along, guiding me with his reassuring style.

I can only image what the world would be like if more of us were encouraged to follow our dreams, as I was by Mike.

The sky's the limit.

DOMESTIC VIOLENCE

As I had learned in using my BB gun, protecting others came naturally to me. Protecting my brother Don's Halloween candy from would-be thieves – like promising to protect my special friend Waddles from harm – displayed a trait I was born with.

As the years went by, our family seemed to be getting smaller with each move. First we moved to Petaluma for two years; our next move was to Van Nuys without my father, whom my mother had recently divorced. Now with another move, from Van Nuys to Reno, Nevada, I lost my brother Jay, who was staying behind in order to settle with a young woman he had met.

Saying my goodbyes, I loaded up my Chevy and convoyed with the family traveling in their car to Reno, which my step dad considered home as well as a location more opportune for his finances. I was hoping all of this uprooting was not going to be the family's new way of life. I was ready to find a stable, lasting place to call home.

Arriving in Reno without securing a place of our own, we found ourselves living with Lloyd's parents, who were renting a three-bedroom, one bath, house north of town. This was not a large home, but it was our only option. I was given the living room area in which to bed down, while my mother and Lloyd occupied one bedroom and my brothers another–not the greatest of conditions, but we managed.

At this point, Lloyd was unemployed and began searching for employment. Besides being out of work, he was looking for a house to rent. By the time he found a suitable house, his personality and demeanor were beginning to shift.

Lloyd was a tall man, heavily built, with short dirty blonde hair and an even shorter temper. When my mother first met him, he had been pleasant and kind, but that soon changed, revealing his true colors – which ran decidedly towards violence.

My brothers Gary and Don took the brunt of his abuse, but my mother was also heavily on the receiving end. No one was exempt from Lloyd's violent behavior. However, at nineteen, my strong constitution prevented him from controlling me as he did the others. I was a fighter and could stand up for myself; I wasn't about to submit to this abusive man.

No one in the family could please Lloyd or even reason with him. The rules he laid down mirrored military life. For example, I couldn't park in the driveway because that space was reserved for his truck (even though there was room for three cars); and no one in the family was allowed to speak of my father. As time went on the rules intensified.

How could this be happening? I thought. Having never experienced a domestic violence situation, I was frightened, unsettled, and at a loss for words. Although my protective instincts had shifted into overdrive, I had no means to change the situation.

My resistance to his violent behavior was like waging war on his so-called manhood. Lloyd forbade

151

any of us to speak about our past or even the things that meant the most to us. He even refused to allow my mother to leave a dinner plate for me in the refrigerator when I arrived home from the job that I had recently acquired.

This situation placed my mother in an agonizing dilemma: feed her daughter, or take the wrath from Lloyd. My mother, like a lion tending to her cubs, hid my food in the refrigerator, out of Lloyd's view, for me to eat when I came home.

The abuse didn't stop there. Don, seven, and Gary, nine, were no match for Lloyd. Taking advantage of their vulnerability, he placed harsh demands on them. Arriving home after working odd jobs, he expected Don and Gary to be waiting at the door like slaves, one with a cup of coffee in hand and the other ready to remove his work boots. Mom and I did our best to ensure that the boys were at their posts daily to perform their "duties."

Late one sunny afternoon, when my mom was out shopping, I heard the rumble of Lloyd's truck pulling into the driveway, a sound I despised as it instantly shifted me into alert mode. I ran to the front door to see if the boys were in their expected place. I saw Gary with Lloyd's cup of coffee in his hand, but Don was nowhere in sight.

"Gary, where is Don?"

Gary's face went pale, eyes widening in fear. "I don't know!"

"I need to find him!" I exclaimed, my heart pounding.

152

Before I could search Don out, Lloyd was already crossing the threshold of the front door. *I'm too late, Lloyd is home.*

"Where's Don?" Lloyd growled.

Gary, doing his best, held out Lloyd's cup of coffee, a slave to his master. My stomach churned in disgust.

In a second Lloyd's face contorted, red, angry, akin to a rabid dog than a human.

"DON, YOU LITTLE PIECE OF CRAP! I'M COMING FOR YOU! AND WHEN I FIND YOU..."
It didn't take him long to find Don in his bedroom, where Lloyd sprang, a snake about to strike – lightning fast, calculated, and deadly. I followed close behind, breathing fast. Trying to reach Don first, I knew my chances were slim.

In a blur, Lloyd pulled Don out of his room, down the hall, into the kitchen – dragging him by his arm so harshly that I was afraid Lloyd was going to rip Don's arm from its socket. Don's small-framed body was no match for Lloyd. The pure terror in Don's face, tears pouring down his cheeks, tore at my heart. I wanted nothing more than to get him away from this evil, sadistic man, but I knew I couldn't. Any help I tried to provide my brothers would only bring them more pain.

Suddenly Gary escaped to my side, silently sobbing. To comfort him, I put my arm around his shoulder, holding him tight. At that point Lloyd commenced with Don's punishment. (Lloyd enjoyed delivering punishments in front of an audience,

153

maximizing embarrassment and degradation, in order to prove a point: follow the rules and obey, or pay the price.)

SMACK! SMACK! Lloyd's hand fell hard and fast on Don's back and buttocks over and over again. There was no escaping the pain and humiliation. Don struggled to maintain his balance on tiptoes as Lloyd's grip imprinted Don's skin. The smacking, mixed with Don's wails reverberating through the house, made me sick to my stomach.

As I watched in horror, Don lost all his strength, knees buckling under him as he collapsed to the floor. I felt that I had fallen with him. Lloyd wasn't deterred; a madman on a mission, he continued his onslaught on Don's body, now curled up on the floor. Suddenly, silence settled over the room, leavened only by Don's pitiful weeping and the pounding of my heart hammering in my ears. Mercifully, the beating finally stopped.

"Playing in your room is not an excuse! Now take off my boots!"

Don, with bruising already visible, rose from the floor, stiff, in pain, snot pouring from his nose. Traumatized and trembling, he began to untie and remove Lloyd's boots. Gary, his brother was trembling with fear beside me, still holding Lloyd's cup of coffee. This was like living in a horror movie that never ends.

Lloyd loomed over Don's battered body. "Will you miss your responsibility again, Don?"

Don, still sobbing, unable to get the words out, merely shook his head.

"Use your words, boy!"

"I wo-won't miss my – my response-responsibility – ag – again – Ll – Lloyd."

Pulsating and blistering through my body, my raging anger was a volcano ready to erupt. I began contriving ways I could dismantle Lloyd -- how I could have him arrested and locked behind bars, where he could no longer ravage my family.

"Go to your room now! And don't you dare leave until I tell you it is okay to come out!"

Fury rolled off my body towards Lloyd like a storm wave hitting the shore – the water murky, fast, hard, and relentless.

Lloyd looked at me in the eyes. "Don't you even think about going to his room!"

Picking up the newspaper, sitting down in his favorite chair, he began reading the paper as if nothing had happened.

I witnessed this sort of abuse for months; I couldn't take it anymore – couldn't take standing silent while my brothers were tormented by this monster. Notifying the police would have held no brief with Lloyd. Laws were still non-existent with respect to domestic violence. It was time for me to take a stand. I had protected Don once using my BB gun against two bullies, and I had protected my special friend Waddles from harm. I was now ready to step up against Lloyd on behalf of my brothers.

My resistance to Lloyd and his way of running a household drew a line in the sand between us. One evening, Gary forgot to move his bike out of the driveway. Lloyd, arriving home, noticed the bike lying on the driveway in the very spot reserved for him. Flinging his truck door open, Lloyd, squinting with anger, spotted Gary playing in the driveway. Lloyd strutted up to him, grabbed him by the left arm, raising him off the ground, dragging him to his bicycle. Gary stood there as Lloyd yelled obscenities, gripping his arm so tight it left a bruise, and forbidding him to ever ride the bike again.

Gary began to cry, trembling with fear. Lloyd picked up a dinner fork lying near the garage door, harpooning it at Gary, with such force that the fork embedded in Gary's right arm. Gary bellowed piteously. I jumped from my chair in the house and ran outside to see what was happening. Lloyd was hovering over Gary as I ran to his aid. In spite of Lloyd's evil squinting eyes and scarlet face, his left hand firmly gripping Gary's arm, I placed my body between them. Lloyd's anger immediately turned toward me.

Lloyd and I wasted no time mincing words, offering Gary a diversion, giving him the opening he needed to flee into the house and hide in his bedroom. Lloyd, unable to silence me, retreated by demanding that I move out. Forcing me to leave was the only power he had over me.
As I was packing my belongings, my mother arrived home and learned of my fate, against which she felt powerless.

I didn't want to leave; I feared for my family. I was a good buffer, and Lloyd knew that. With me gone, he could have a field day with them.

Having no other choice and nowhere to go, I called my sister, Ana, who was still living in Petaluma. Ana and Cosimo opened their door to me. I returned to Petaluma and quickly found a job – a boring job, in which I worked a graveyard position for a diode chip maker. My pay was decent but far from my dreams. I felt frustrated and angry, but I was still as determined as ever to achieve my dreams.

I thought of my mother and brothers, my heart breaking each time I imagined what they might be going through. My distress was amplified by having been forbidden by Lloyd to contact my mother. As much as I wanted to call, I didn't do so in fear of the repercussions my mother and brothers would experience if Lloyd found out.

One night, a year after I left Reno, I had a disturbing dream, in which I was walking in a cemetery, grieving over my mother's grave. I was standing near a decayed old oak tree when her hand shot up through the dirt and grabbed my arm. I could hear her voice cry out.

"I need you Teresa! Where are you? Come back!"

Awakening from the dream sweating and distraught, I knew I needed to call my mother regardless of Lloyd. This was a sign. I waited until the morning, when I hoped and prayed that my mother, rather than Lloyd, would answer the phone.

Ring. Ring. Ring. Come on mom pick up the phone.

On the fifth ring, I heard her voice

157

"Hello?"

I had been holding my breath the whole time.

"Mom, its Teresa, how are you?"

"Oh, Teresa, I am so glad you called. How are you?"

"I'm good. I had this strange dream about you last night. Are you okay? Is something going on?" (A jittery sound in my voice).

After a few moments of silence, my mother sighed, "I am pregnant."

"What?" I was shocked.

Given my mom's age, giving birth was dangerous. At forty two years old she was warned by the doctors of the problems that could occur. With the husband and father that I knew Lloyd to be, I feared for her and her unborn child. I made a decision that moment.

"Mom, I will be on my way."

A few months passed before Al was born in May of 1974, Lloyd's only child. Given my experience with Lloyd, I feared that Al's future would surely bring him torment and loneliness. I was twenty years older than Al, and I felt compelled to protect him.

As Al grew older, Lloyd grew more violent towards him in response to everything he did. Al was so young, and my mother couldn't protect herself, let alone him.

I did my best to shield both my mother and brothers from Lloyd. It was a nightmare. I wasn't totally spared from his sadistic behavior, but I was on a mission to protect the family. When my friends came over to the house, they often observed Lloyd's behavior, pleading with me to move out of this abusive home; but I couldn't leave my family behind. It was love, not fear, that caused me to stay.

In the meantime, I had been accepted to the Sheriff's Department Police Academy, offering me considerable positive reinforcement. By the time I had graduated from the Academy, I had gained a better understanding of the law, from which I learned that the law was completely mute on domestic violence. I learned through my training that the term *domestic violence* was still not even heard of, and laws were nonexistent for victims of it. It was enraging to know that that man, if you can call him that, had more rights and protection than my mother and brothers.

One night, Lloyd and I got into a particularly angry altercation about law enforcement. Lloyd proceeded to correct me on the law and our training, subjects he knew nothing about. Our voices rose in mutual hostility, but I was not backing down. Not this time.

"GET OUT OF MY HOUSE!" He roared, just as he did previously when he knew I was standing my ground. We stood there glaring at each other.

"Lloyd, please!" My mother sobbed behind him.

"Shut up, Jean,"

I could see his anger turning towards my mom, and I knew this wasn't a fight I could win. He took a few steps closer to her, to which she began shrinking back. By this time, I was aghast at the thought of my mother taking the heat for my fight.

"All right! All right! I'll leave!"

Lloyd turned toward me.

"You have two hours to get your stuff and get out!"

I could still hear my mother sobbing quietly.

"Fine!"

Turning on my heel, I headed to my room, my anger radiating like a blast furnace. I trembled slightly as I began tossing my things into black plastic trash bags, which served as the closest approximation to luggage that I happened to own.

I was surprised that it took Lloyd five years to kick me out a second time! He clearly wanted to break me; I was a challenge he needed to overcome. He must have realized that that conquest wasn't ever going to happen, so he did the one thing he knew he *could* do: he took my family from me.

"Teresa?"

I heard a small voice behind me. It was my baby brother, Al; he had no doubt heard the fight between Lloyd and me.

"Hey, Al," I said softly. "What are you doing out of bed?"

Cowering in the corner, Al sobbed, "Are you leaving?"

Hearing this plaintive question, I was heartsick. In my anger I had forgotten for a moment how hard this change would be on him.

"Yes, Buddy, I am. I have to."

His eyes grew wide in fear as his crying intensified.

"No! No! No, please, you can't leave me! PLEASE don't leave me!"

My heart was shattering. Suddenly I was fighting against the overwhelming feeling of drowning in my own helplessness.

I kept my voice as calm as I could. "Al, I have no choice. This is your dad's house. I have no say in whether I stay or go. I have to leave. I am so sorry, Buddy."

"No! Please no!"

By now Al backed himself into the corner near my bedroom door

"I'm gonna die if you leave me here alone."

He whispered through his tears. The sight of Al huddled into a sobbing ball left a lasting scar.

161

After my allotted two hours had expired, I headed for the front door. Al ran after me, and I hugged him as tight as I could. He clung to me as if I were his last lifeline.

"Come here, Al. Now!" Al reluctantly let go of me and ran, still sniffling, to stand near his father.

It was heart-wrenching to see Al so helpless and vulnerable to Lloyd's wrath. Glaring at Lloyd, I walked out the door.

In spite of my anger and humiliation, I left that house with a firm resolve: I would never allow a man like Lloyd in my life. He had clearly shown me what a man is NOT, and I vowed that I would never traffic with anyone capable of such cruelty.

Several years passed before I received a call from my mother. She was ready to leave her abusive relationship with Lloyd, asking if I could help her move. Having planned the perfect time to help pack her belongings when Lloyd was not home, I drove to her house. After packing my truck with her belongings as fast as I could, I whisked my mother and Al to safer quarters in the form of a newly rented apartment.

Having effectively left Lloyd behind, my mother went on to reinvent herself. In the following years she earned a degree in corporate finance, gaining the self-sufficiency to raise her son in a healthier environment. Her well-deserved freedom allowed her to heal and grow in spite of everything that she had been through.

As for me, standing strong against Lloyd's violent and bullying ways took a lot out of me, both physically and mentally. However, I had made it clear to him that I wasn't bowing to his abuse, just as I had done as a child in dealing with a surpassingly cruel, emerging bully named Vivian.

THE FIRST WOMAN HIRED

Returning to Reno for the second time, prior to being kicked out for good, I knew I had to get a job to help support my family. Lloyd was the main breadwinner, but I was determined to be independent as soon as possible. My dreams and passion for working in law enforcement and auto mechanics continued to grow every day, and, while I didn't know how I was going to carve out my path, I was determined to progress nonetheless.

Shortly thereafter, I found a job through a temporary agency as an accounts receivable clerk for a dog food manufacturing company. It could not have been further from what I wanted to pursue; but it paid well, and I needed a job.

The office personnel working at the dog food plant were female -- no surprise, really, as these were traditional jobs for women. The ladies there were wonderful, and I quickly became friends with many of them. I even earned the nickname of "Quills" when one co-worker had a difficult time pronouncing my last name of "Aquila," so "quills" I happily became.

Since it was a manufacturing plant, there was a maintenance shop on location. I held secret hopes that I might one day be able to move into a position in the shop rather than in the office.

One day on the company bulletin board, I noticed a posted opening in the shop for an apprentice mechanic. Knowing it might be a long shot, I immediately applied. I made it my mission to be the person to fill the position. Immediately, I sought out the general manager about applying for the opening.

"Sir, I see that there is an opening for an apprentice mechanic and I would like to apply." I was sure my excitement was obvious.

The manager looked at me as though I were crazy.

"You're kidding, right? This is not a job for a girl; this is a man's job," he asserted, laughing and shaking his head in disbelief.

"No, I'm not kidding. I would like to apply for the position."

Gathering his thoughts, he stared at me for a few seconds.

"In the history of this plant, no woman has ever occupied that position. It is not a place for a female," he said, walking off, still chuckling to himself.

This response did not rest well with me.

To me, this was no laughing matter; it was serious, and I was serious about applying. As a result, I became like gum on his shoe. I stuck to him every day, asking for a chance at the position.

After weeks of constant importuning, I was surprised when the manager approached my desk early one morning.

"Teresa, I have sent a request to our corporate office for consideration to allow a woman in the shop. I am not sure if they will consider it, but I will let you know when I receive their recommendations."

"Thank you." I was shocked and surprised. I guessed my persistence had paid off.

Two weeks later, I received a phone call from the corporate office.

"Hi, Teresa, my name is Justin from Corporate Human Resources. My curiosity has gotten the better of me, and I want to know why you are seeking the apprentice mechanic position in the Sparks plant shop."

"Well, I have wanted to be a mechanic ever since I was a little girl. It is a passion I have always had. This is not a passing phase or something I just want to try. This is what I want to do with my life. I want to be a mechanic, and starting as an apprentice would be a great opportunity."

"This has always been a man's job and very hard work. Are you up for all that comes with it? The long hours, the climbing, lifting and thinking fast on your feet?"

It dawned on me that he must believe women knew nothing of these things, nor could they do them.

"Yes, I am. I have thought about this long and hard for years, and this is where my heart is. I know I can perform the duties if given the chance." I hoped my passion was obvious.

After calling me several times, Human Resources had decided that my interest in this opening reflected passion and confidence. To my excitement, they offered me the position. My path was opening up, my dreams were taking form, and I was on Cloud Nine. Little did I expect what I would encounter from the majority of the male shop mechanics . . .

As a mechanic, I was required to bring my own tools. However, the company allowed the employees to build their own basic toolbox out of scrap steel found in the shop. Wanting to be as prepared as possible for my first day, I went down to the shop ahead of time in order to build my toolbox.

Laying out the needed material, I cut the pieces to size and then realized, never having welded before, that I was going to need some assistance. I sought out a fellow mechanic in hopes that he would offer me some guidance. I approached one of the mechanics sweeping the floor.

"Hello?"

"Yeah?" He said as he turned to face me.

"Hello, my name is Teresa; I am the new mechanic's apprentice," holding out my hand.

His eyebrows rose up, and he looked quite surprised. *Oh great* I thought, *He is probably going to lecture me on why this is no job for a woman.* To my surprise, he didn't. Instead, he extended his hand in a friendly handshake.

167

"Hello, Teresa, I'm John. Welcome to the team." He reminded me of Mike in Van Nuys, who had no problem in accepting me as mechanic either.

John, a long-time company employee, was clearly more than happy to help me. I was able, with John's help, to get my toolbox fully built by the end of my shift; but it still needed a paint job. That would have to wait until the following Monday morning.

Starting my first day in the shop on that Monday made me both excited and nervous as I headed to my toolbox awaiting its paint job. That is when I saw it: it was already sporting fresh paint.

The paint color on the box was far from traditional. Instead of a solid red, blue or green, mine had been adorned in white with pink polka-dots and finished off with a pretty pink bow on the front. (Anyone who couldn't see that this box belonged to a woman had to be color-blind.) Had the box been painted by someone who accepted me in the shop? Or was it their version of war paint?

That morning brought a meeting, intended to introduce me to the rest of the crew and lay out the day's workload. Before heading to the meeting, I placed my tools in my newly painted toolbox.

When I entered the room, the air was thick with tension. I felt eyes glaring at me and heard mumbled disapprovals under the breath of some of the men. As I took the first available seat, I said to no one in particular, "Thank you to whoever painted my toolbox for me; the colors are perfect" – eliciting a few snickers from around the room.

168

How naive was I to have thought that I would be accepted? Taking a deep breath, I knew this crew would try to get me worked up – maybe even cry – but they did not know me at all. It was going to take a lot more than a paint job to break me. Besides, I liked the color pink. It might be considered a girly color; but, honestly, what is there not to like about it? That it is associated with the female sex? Well, so be it. Right then and there I embraced my pink and white toolbox.

At this point, the shop foreman began assigning different jobs and projects. As a new employee, I was required to shadow a mechanic for my first two weeks to train and learn the ropes.

"All right, the last thing on the agenda for today: everyone, this is Teresa, our new mechanic's apprentice." This announcement was met by dead silence; not even the foreman himself welcomed me.

"She needs to shadow one of you to get the lay of the land. Any takers?"

I couldn't believe the foreman was handling the situation in this manner. Instead of simply assigning me to someone, he obviously wanted to highlight how unwanted I was in the shop. He clearly wanted me to feel small. But I refused to sink into my chair or show any emotions.

"Sure, she can shadow me," a voice behind me said.

I turned to see who it was. It was John. Out of all the mechanics, he was the only one willing to accept a woman in his workspace.

I could feel the surprise in the air and see it on our foreman's face. "All right, then," he said, clearing his throat. I am sure that he had bet on no one wanting to work with me.

From that day forward, each day was challenging in trying to prove myself as a mechanic to those insistent that a woman's place was not in their shop but at home as a wife. They were adamant against change, and I represented just that. Being a trailblazer and first to venture into untouched territory for women, I was presenting a challenge to both sides.

I wasn't there because I wanted to be part of a movement; I was there to earn a living and be part of a career I wanted. Most of my male co-workers could not see that – all these men saw was a woman infiltrating their sacred grounds.

The attempted desecration of my toolbox was only the beginning. At first the harassment started out with small sabotages to my work, making me look incompetent to our foreman. Work I had finished they would either completely undo or change an element or two, creating the appearance that I had done it incorrectly.

Further, they often verbally assaulted me, making snide, belittling comments. Unfortunately, the foreman never stepped in by way of response, and the only occasions when I received any kind of reprieve from these men occurred when I was working with John and

Warren, who had also become my friend and had accepted me.

One day in spring, about a month after I started working in the shop, we experienced an issue with the sprinkler systems in the form of a broken pipe. I was assigned with two others, Stan and Harry, to locate the pipe and replace it. We grabbed our shovels and headed out to fix the problem.

Now, Stan had always made it known to me that he did not appreciate my presence in the shop. Harry, however, was quiet; he never spoke to me. Instead, I would often find him staring at me, giving me an uncomfortable feeling.

We were able to locate the broken pipe because of a flooded area in the lawn. I began to dig when I noticed my "team" was just standing there, obviously unwilling to help. I ignored them and kept on digging until I was within sight of the broken pipe. Bending over to clear out the rest of the dirt, I was facing the sun. Suddenly, I sensed something or someone blocking the sun's warmth. In the same instant, I was shocked to feel the calloused hand of a man reaching down the front of my shirt towards my breast. I looked up to see Harry trying to grope me.

I was having none of it! Anger quickly erupted within me. One of my hands grabbed his wrist to stop him from reaching his desired objective, while my other one quickly latched onto my shovel next to me. Raising the tool, I shoved the blade in front of Harry's face while pushing his violating hand back towards him.

"The next time you or anyone else in the group tries this, my shovel will be up your ass so fast it will come out your nose." Livid, I now had a solid two-hand grip on my shovel. Harry's face revealed his shock.

Stan started to laugh. "Looks like you hit a button, Harry," he snickered, no doubt amused by our interaction.

At this point, I turned the shovel towards him. "Do I make myself clear?" I seethed.

"Yeah, yeah. Take it down a notch, will ya?" Stan replied, hands in the air.

For good measure, I turned the shovel back toward Harry, who had backed up a few steps.

"I found the pipe. You guys can fix it." I walked away, needing some space. How dare these men think they could violate me?

When we returned to the shop, the story got around pretty quickly. That was the last time these cretins tried that stunt, but it wasn't the end of their attempt to get me to quit and free their shop of a woman. However, I never went to the boss and complained. I handled it my way, knowing that if the situation further deteriorated I would have to report the problem.

In any case, I stayed focused on my duties, learning everything I could, no matter the job assigned. I was there to grow, and I knew this job was only going to be a stepping-stone for me.

One day I was assigned to clean out the grain silo's filters – a job disliked by everybody, and with good reason. It was more dangerous, scary, and unpleasant than I realized at the time.

"Hey, now you're playing with big boys. Think you can handle it?" Stan inquired, as I prepared for the job.

"Shut up, Stan!" John demanded, glaring at Stan.

"You've got this," John reassured me.

"Hey, if you fall, don't worry. Someone will find you eventually!" Stan continued with his jabbing. Everyone else joined in with laughter and their own hurtful comments.

"Ignore them," John said, again addressing me.

As if on cue, one of the guys shouted, "Hey, Teresa, it's okay if you quit and go home to your mommy!" But I had no intention of backing out. What bothered me most was that these men felt no shame in trivializing my life and safety.

The job consisted of climbing to the top of the eighty-foot silo, entering through an access door, and traversing a narrow catwalk while cleaning filters heavy with dirt. OSHA not having been established at the time, there were no safety rails, no nets, and no harnesses. I was on my own.

The dust from the filters was suffocating; wearing a face mask was imperative. Feeling pressure to prove I could perform this job, I handled it with grace and extreme caution. One wrong move and I could end up in the grain – never to be seen again until the silo was emptied.

I steeled my nerves, focused on my task, never looking down, while blocking out the taunting voices of my so-called fellow workers as they continued with their jabs and insults. Even with all of the distractions and lack of support, I nailed it. I did my job and did it well. As I climbed down from the silo, I was greeted with annoyed grunts of frustration. I just took a breath, smiled, and proceeded to my next assignment.

About three weeks after the sprinkler incident, I noticed one of my co-workers, Steve, starting to take an interest in me. My instincts told me that his actions and attempts at friendship were not genuine. He was a far cry from John and Warren, and up until that point he had never shown a glimmer of support for me or my presence in the shop.

After a few days of small talk and trying to warm me up to him, he asked, "Hey, want to go to my cabin this weekend? It is great – private. We can have a lot of fun." His arrogance oozed off him.

"Well, Steve, no," I said, as I continued to work, avoiding his gaze. "How much money are you going to lose?"

"Excuse me?" he asked.

"Oh, please, as if I don't know you have a bet going on with at least five other guys that you can get into my pants."

I stopped working in order to look at him.

174

"What? No," he said trying to play it cool.

"Looks like you lose. I hope it breaks your bank," I said. I was not there to hook up with a man; I was there to develop my career.

At the time (the late '70s), any indication that a woman might even be considered "promiscuous" was a sure-fire path to the destruction of her reputation and career. Steve had tried this gambit and failed.

As my time with this company progressed, it became apparent that everything about me was on trial every day. From my gender and my abilities, to my determination to stay, I had entered a daily test of my will.

This challenge was taking a toll, and I was feeling exhausted. My stress levels rose to the stratospheric. Between dealing with Lloyd at home and the jerks at the plant, I was on the ropes. Still, I went to work every day to face the hostility all over again.

"Teresa, we need to talk," said John one morning when I arrived at the shop. Warren was at his side.

"Okay," I replied.

His intense tone instantly told me this was serious; I had no idea what to expect. John was always laid back and got along with everyone; why would he be so grave? But, since he was my dear friend, I knew that what he had to tell me was important.

"After you left yesterday, Warren and I ended up in a fight with a few of our co-workers," he explained.

175

"Okay. Why? What happened?"

"It doesn't matter; you don't need to know all the details but..."

"What?"

"But it had to do with you. A few of the guys were tampering with your work."

"Well, that's nothing new," I responded.

"I know, but this was different. Warren and I witnessed it first-hand and took them out back to try to talk sense into them."

John went on to explain that he and Warren informed them in so many words – and fists – that, thereafter, anyone in the shop who touched or tampered with my work could expect major repercussions. Further, if any sabotage of my work were to cause harm, he would make sure the offender would end up at the bottom of a grain silo, not to be found for days.

I was surprised and shocked. Whatever John and Warren had witnessed had to have been horrendous. This severe action was out of character for both him and Warren. I took him very seriously.

"John, thank you. Thank you for standing up for what is right, not just for me." I was still flabbergasted.

To this day, I still don't know what my co-workers had done to prompt John and Warren to stand up for me. I only knew that their behavior had to have been horrific.

In any case, John was a true friend then and for many years to follow. He was one of the few who gave me faith and hope that there were other men in the world who would stand up for justice and fairness. He clearly was one of them, and I will be forever grateful for his friendship.

In spite of John and Warren's support, the continuing conflict over my presence at the plant made it plain to me that it was time for me to move on. I needed to find a new job – *soon*.

AUTOMOTIVE BOUND

Thoroughly disaffected with the dog food plant, I began pounding the job market for my next employer. I knew I couldn't tender my resignation at Spice Island until I had a new source of income lined up; I had rent and bills to pay. I scoured the classifieds section of all the local newspapers daily, hoping to find work. I wasn't having much luck until an opportunity crossed my path in an unexpected way.

It was 1978, and I still had my first car, the white Chevy. She was my baby, and I made sure to keep her maintained in tip-top condition. When I needed parts or supplies for the car, I went to Grand Auto Parts and Service Center, one of only a few auto parts stores in the area. During my frequent visits to the store, I made friends with Bev, the cashier, who seemed to admire me for being a woman who knew how to work on her own car.

During one of these visits to the store, Bev excitedly informed me that the store was looking for a parts person; she wasted not a minute in encouraging me to apply. The timing could not have been better: not only did I want out of Spice Island; I was also trying to find my way into automotive repair. Matching Bev's enthusiasm, I readily accepted the application that she presented to me, asking me to return it to her so that she could make a pitch to the store manager on my behalf.

I was a little nervous about going from being a factory mechanic to a parts counter person, but I knew I had to try. Returning the following afternoon, I gave Bev my application.

"Wait here," Bev instructed.

She disappeared into the back of the store, returning a few minutes later with the manager, Ken. After appropriate introductions, we exchanged pleasantries for a moment.

Ken seemed sincere – a nice change from dealing with Melton, the toad, on a regular basis. Ken reviewed my qualifications, asking me a few questions. The next thing I knew, he had offered me the job on the spot! Wow – I was positively blown away that he didn't even want to check my references. I accepted the job, feeling a huge weight lifted from my shoulders; no longer would I have to deal with Melton.

At the same time, my duties at the Sheriff's Department were also taking shape. I had graduated from the Academy as a Category One deputy and was moving on to the practical training. Both of my childhood dreams were really coming together. I still had my work cut out for me, but my future was looking bright.

Working at Grand Auto was a much needed change and, thankfully, I didn't receive much resistance from my co-workers for being a woman. Interestingly enough, I did, however, receive resistance from some of the customers. One particularly memorable incident that stands out in my memories actually came from a woman.

It was a quiet afternoon in the store when a female customer walked in and came straight to the parts counter where I was working.

"Good afternoon," I greeted her.

"Good afternoon. I need some parts for my red car out there," she said, pointing to the parking lot outside. She must have thought I had x-ray vision, because, for one thing, I couldn't see the parking lot; secondly, her description "red car" gave me little to go on.

"Okay – no problem," I offered, what is the make and model of your vehicle?"

Eyes suddenly narrowing, she looked me up and down as if just realizing she was speaking to a woman. "Do you have any men that work here? I would prefer to talk to someone who knows what he's doing," she demanded, clearly irritated.

Ignoring her rudeness, I replied, "I don't have any male parts people on duty today, but I do have a few stock boys in the back."

"Get me one of them," she insisted. In response, I activated the PA system and asked for a stocker to please come to the parts counter. When Bobby, still a senior in high school, arrived, he asked me if I needed help.

"No, but the lady here does." I responded. "She would prefer to speak to a male in regard to the parts she is looking for." Bobby gave me a confused look but turned to the waiting customer anyway.

"Hello," she stated "I need parts for my red car, please."

Bobby looked at me again, confused, before asking, "Um, okay what kind of car do you have?"

(I have to admit that I was somewhat enjoying this exchange as I knew that Bobby wouldn't be able to help her in the end. But she wanted a boy, and she *got* a boy.)

"Really?" she asked. "Is there no one that knows what he's doing?"

"Ma'am, I'm sorry, but I know nothing about cars. I'm just a stocker. Teresa here is our parts specialist. If anyone can help you, she can," he said.

Obviously disliking this statement, the customer huffed, "I'll figure it out myself," as she walked off.

"What was that all about?" Bobby asked me.

"That is what happens when someone believes a woman cannot do what they think is a man's job," I answered.

"That's not cool," he said.

"No, it isn't. Don't be one of those people, Bobby," I mentored, hoping to steer a young male's mind away from prejudice against women.

Fifteen minutes later, the lady was still wandering up and down the aisles as I noticed her moving closer to the counter again. As I watched her out of the corner of my eye, I said to myself, *She truly believes that because I am a woman I could not possibly have any automotive knowledge.*

That is when it dawned on me. "*Of course* that is what she thinks. She herself knows nothing about cars;

she didn't even know the make and model of her own vehicle."

In that moment, I realized she had been deflecting her insecurities along with her ignorance on to me. I felt bad for her. I decided to approach her and offer my assistance one last time.

"Excuse me, ma'am? If you don't mind taking me outside to see your car, I'm sure I could help you get the parts you need," I offered.

After a moment's appraisal of my intentions, she gave in. "It's right out here," she said.

After seeing her car and discovering that the problem was an electrical issue, I was able to help her get the exact parts she needed. In the end, she seemed extremely grateful and became a longtime customer, seeking me out whenever she came in.

I learned a valuable lesson that afternoon. I learned how to work with customers – instead of merely transacting business with them. It can be hard to step away from how people treat you, (especially if they clearly consider you to be "different") and focus instead on how you can help them. I discovered that when I worked on improving myself, rather than trying to *prove* myself, I had a far more positive impact. Presently, I became well known at Grand Auto, and soon many customers were asking for me by name. There was always a customer or two that had issues with my being a woman so knowledgeable in parts and automotive repair; but I never let their bias bother me, and most of the time they saw that I was the woman for the job.

I spent eight years working for Grand Auto – a period during which I gained invaluable experience in auto parts, automotive repair, and business methods. It was also a time of personal growth for me as a deputy sheriff as well. The gains from both of my passions were molding me into a different person – a person whose pride and self-confidence were growing every day. I was coming out of my shell within the sheriff's department as well as Grand Auto, my shy defensive mechanism crumbling away as I realized it no longer served me.

However, after those eight years at Grand Auto, I was becoming bored and restless. I still craved a more hands-on job in automotive repair. After all that time with this company, I had only progressed from parts person to assistant manager, while my male co-workers were being quickly promoted to manager; if that was not a clear sign of stagnation, nothing else would be.

When I joined Grand Auto, I wasn't pursuing the objective of moving up within the company, even when men with far less experience or knowledge became my managers. At the time, this wasn't a hill I was willing to die on. Instead, I chose to move on.

It was a good thing I did so, because the biggest fight of my life was yet to come.

BAREFOOT, PREGNANT, AND IN THE KITCHEN

In my continuing desire to leave Grand Auto, I longed to find a mechanical position in which I could do more hands-on work in automotive repair. Soon I found a company new to the Reno/Sparks area but well-known in the automotive world: Porsche Cars North America, which was looking to open two new pre-delivery inspection (PDI) facilities and warehouses in the US.

When I heard this news, I jumped at the opportunity and submitted my application and resume immediately. To my excitement, I found myself honored with an invitation to interview with the director of maintenance, Dave Martin.

The company's new PDI center was still being built during their hiring process, as they wanted to ensure they had a full staff on board before their opening day, for which they were interviewing applicants for the entire facility. My own interview went well, and the director seemed to be the type of man who was more interested in employees' qualifications than in their gender.

Two days after the interview, I was notified that I had indeed landed a job as a shop technician. To me, this was amazing; it was my first real opportunity to work in a mechanical shop – and for a distinguished company to boot. This was truly the day my dream of becoming a mechanic became a reality

One impressive aspect of working for Porsche Cars North America was that they (unlike most shops)

supplied the mechanics with all the necessary tools for performing their duties. My toolbox and its contents, a mechanics dream, cost more than I made in almost a year. Without those tools it would have been considerably more difficult to execute the work. It made sense that the company spoiled us in that manner; it benefited them as much as the mechanics.

During the first two weeks, things were going rather well for me and my position with the company. However, this was the mid-eighties, and women were still not accepted in the automotive world. A prime example of that resistance was presented by one co-worker in particular, Adam. Extremely knowledgeable in foreign vehicles and highly qualified for his position, he wanted no part of working with females.

Adam and I were hired at the same time, so it wasn't as if he wasn't aware of a woman's presence in the shop. But he was definitely opposed to it. In that sense, he appeared to be rather typical, apparently wondering how a real woman would want to work with tools and get her hands dirty. Doesn't that mess up her fingernail polish? Women don't have the mind to fix things; they bake things; and so on. With an attitude like that, it didn't take Adam long to advance into making my days miserable.

My daily work consisted of half the day on the production line, the other half focused on operating the dynamometer. (A device which uses the cars spinning rear wheels to test for proper vehicle performance. The cars either passed or were rejected for further work.)

During my hours on the production line, Adam would spare no words as to how much he despised my presence in the shop. When, for example, he double-checked my work to make sure that I had done it correctly, I knew he was actually hoping to find something he could get me fired over.

With in a month, Adam's behavior had become so intense – and so unreasonable – that I had no choice but to completely ignore him. After all, this wasn't my first rodeo. I had already dealt with men like Adam, and so I chose to pretend he wasn't even there. (Unless, of course, work necessitated interacting with him.) Even if he tried to engage in idle talk, I ignored him. He made my days more stressful than needed, and he was wasting time furthering intolerance instead of teamwork. His stubbornness and insecurities were exhausting.

It wasn't until the President of Porsche Cars North America sent the facility a 1970 Chevy Chevelle Convertible for restoration that Adam showed his true colors to others besides me. This was the President's personal vehicle and was to receive priority and top-notch work. I was assigned some of the mechanical duties, under the direction of Adam, for this project. I bit my tongue and dove into my work.

One day, when Adam was off sick, the PDI director asked me to reassemble the doors on the Chevy. He needed them installed and a few repairs to the interior completed so that the car could be painted. I obliged, even though I suspected that Adam was going to be steamed. This particular area had been assigned to him. However, I was not one to question my supervisor's instructions that I fill in for Adam, and I therefore proceeded to tackle the job. I examined all of the parts, laid everything out to insure I had all that was needed to complete the installation, and by day's end had finished the job.

The next day, Adam arrived expecting to finish the President's car. When he noticed he had been assigned other duties for the day, he asked the director how the car's doors had been installed, to which question he was informed that I had been given the task and completed it.

Of course, Adam immediately had to check my work. *Oh, great,* I thought. *Here we go again.* I assumed that after his "inspection" I would be getting an earful. But, to my surprise, I didn't see him until later that morning.

At midmorning break time, I headed up to the break room and sat down to read the newspaper. Two minutes later, I could see from the corner of my eye Adam shuffling in, looking distressed.

"Teresa, may I sit?" he asked, motioning to the chair across the table from me. I was puzzled by his uncharacteristic politeness.

"It's a free country," I replied, not even bothering to look up from the newspaper.

"Teresa I —" He took a deep breath, hesitating and appearing nervous. I could hear the struggle in his voice, sense it with his energy. Still, I kept reading my newspaper. "I have been a jerk to you," he finally declared.

This sudden admission caused me to abruptly set down the paper.

"*What?*" I asked. He was looking straight at me.

"I owe you an apology," he said, looking stricken. "In all the years that I have been turning wrenches I have never worked with a woman who knew how to repair and restore cars," he explained. I was shocked. This was the last thing I was expecting to hear coming out of Adam's mouth.

"Oh, have you worked with many women?"

"No."

"So, on the basis of no previous experience whatsoever, you just assumed I couldn't do the job. Why? Because I'm a woman?"

I wasn't going to let him off easy. I wanted him to understand how absurd his beliefs had been.

"Yeah, yes. Like I said, I was a jerk. You did an amazing job on the door installation and interior repairs." He stuck his hand out as a peace offering. I took it, and to our surprise we agreed to a fresh start. It was a first for both of us.

From that moment on, Adam and I were a team – and a really good one. During the next year and a half, things were going well for us at Porsche Cars North America – that is, until a new director was hired.

Enter Shane. He was hired as our new director after our previous one had recently been promoted. From day one, he made himself more than clear as to how he felt having a female mechanic in his shop.

During the director's first day, I was performing some repairs on a car with Adam when Shane walked straight up to me, holding a clipboard.

"Teresa Aquila, right?"

"Yes sir," I replied. I had a feeling this wasn't going to be good.

"I am just going to be completely honest with you, Teresa. I don't want you in my shop. This is no place for a woman."

He started to walk away, but turned back and stated smugly, "In fact, the only place a woman belongs is barefoot, pregnant and in the kitchen." Appearing satisfied, he walked off.

I couldn't believe he had actually said that to me. Wow. He had made it clear that he believed women were nothing but property for men -- weak and helpless while serving men and giving them babies.

Well, not this woman.

I wanted to tell him off, but I highly doubted that it would do any good. It was at that point that I knew my days at Porsche Cars North America were numbered, especially after Shane pulled me from the shop and reassigned me to the production line. (To his annoyance and frustration, he couldn't pull me from the dynamometer yet, as there were still only two of us trained to run it.)

I tried to work with Shane as best I could, but it was impossible and futile. One evening, I became very ill, and, after work the next day, I went to the doctor. I was told to go home and stay in bed for a day or two. I had caught a nasty flu virus and was sporting a fever of 103. I was given a note from the doctor recommending a few days off.

The next morning, still with a fever of 103, and aware that calling in sick was a poor idea, I dragged myself into work to give Shane the doctor's note in person. I did not want to give him any fuel for his fire to rid me of my job.

Feeling beyond miserable, I handed Shane the doctor's note. I just wanted to go home, crawl into bed, and sleep this flu off. To my shock and horror, I watched, my brain fever-muddled, as he ripped the note to shreds, up close, in front of my face.

"Get to work. If not, you're fired," he demanded.

"Are you kidding me?" I asked incredulously. "I am sick. It isn't safe for me to be working,"

"Does it look like I care?" He replied expressionlessly.

Every inch of my body wanted to retaliate against his enjoyment of his power over me, but I swallowed my pride. I had bills to pay. I lived on my own; quitting was not an option. Making matters worse, my fevered brain and body were in no shape to fight, no matter how much I wanted to.

With no better available alternatives, I used my anger and determination to fuel myself as I was forced to go to work. I pushed myself as much as I could; but eventually my body gave out. It was during the second half of the day, when I was working the dynamometer, that I almost passed out due to my high fever, causing the car being tested, to nearly swerve off the machine. This near mishap led a few of my co-workers to assert that I should go home.

At that point I realized how ludicrous the situation was. My life was more important than this job. *What are you doing?* I thought, and, without another thought, I walked out. I went home.

At home recuperating from the flu for the next two days, I received a phone call from my sergeant at the Sheriff's office, Dan Daly. "Hey, I wanted to let you know that your director, Shane, from Porsche, has been calling me every day since you have been sick, asking me if you have been reporting to duty. I don't know what his problem is, but I let him know that you have been out sick."

I merely thanked him, too tired to explain the situation to him. Besides, there wasn't anything he could do anyway.

So Shane was checking up on me, as if I were lying.

After three days out sick, I was able to return to work. The second I appeared, Shane was on me like a hawk.

"Come to my office, Teresa," he ordered. "Since you decided to miss work, I'm writing you up for a no-show," he stated.

191

I was livid. "Excuse me, but I had a doctor's note, called in everyday I was unable to come in, and I was clearly sick," I said, keeping my voice calm and even, stating the facts.

"Don't play innocent with me. I called the Sheriff's Department, and they told me you were scheduled,"

"Yes, I was scheduled, but I was unable to report to duty,"

"Right!", That's why Lisa and Barbara from the office both said you stopped by in your patrol car to say hello to them." he announced, aiming his malevolent Boris Karloff grin at me.

I couldn't believe Shane would go so far as to make up lies to further his false case against me – not to mention that he knew it would put the two office ladies in a bad position. He really was a horror of a human being.

"Okay, sign here to show you have received and reviewed your written warning," he instructed, shoving a clipboard toward me.

"No," I said firmly.

"Excuse me?'

"No," I said again. Looking him straight in the eye. "I am not going to sign something that is untrue and full of lies,"

"Well, then, you give me no choice but to bring this problem to the attention of my supervisor and Human Resources." He was gleaming in satisfaction.

Unfortunately, in the end, Human Resources allowed the write-up to be placed into my employee file. It was at this time that Shane was able to change my assignment yet again. I was now on battery duty – each car arriving at the PDI center would get a freshly charged battery.

This was extremely repetitive physical work, twisting, tweaking, lifting, and pulling each 40 lb battery in every car. My motions never varied, as I repeated them over and over, without change-up, or reprieve – contrary to our previous director's expectations that we switch out jobs and move around.

Working 10 hour shifts, my body paid the price. After about two months, my arm began to hurt and became weak. I was in constant pain but worked through it nonetheless.

It wasn't until the pain reached levels of agony in my neck, shoulder, and arm that I finally gave in and went to the ER. An x-ray revealed that because of the long repetitious hours, I had ruptured a disc in my neck.

Accordingly, I filed a worker's compensation claim, which was accepted. However, I had to leave my job in order for my injury to heal or immediately undergo surgery to repair the rupture – which meant that Shane ultimately got what he wanted: my departure as his employee.

The one reality that Shane failed to diminish or damage was my spirit, my determination, and my passion. No one could take that away from me.

Life Inside the Boys' Club

After leaving Porsche, I landed a mechanic's job at the local school district's maintenance facility. The District was currently adding a swing shift with six new mechanics; I was hired as one of the six. Still having problems with the disc in my neck, I still managed to perform my mechanical duties, although I had to adjust to a new way of performing my job. Not long after taking the job, I was scheduled to undergo surgery for a fusion in my neck.

In spite of my injury, I was excited about my new position as a heavy duty mechanic. This was a turning point, not just for me but for women in general. Holding the position of first female diesel mechanic came with a heavy weight on my shoulders. I embraced that responsibility, and I hoped to learn from some of the seasoned mechanics in order to advance my knowledge in diesel repair.

From day one, my co-workers received me with little other than open hostility – my work constantly sabotaged in an effort to discredit me.

On one occasion, one of the other mechanics came up to me and said right to my face, "You are taking money out of a man's wallet."

"Really? So who is filling mine?" I shot back. He turned and walked away.

The first week on the job was a bit rocky, as the other mechanics tried to size me up and determine if I was really suited for this line of work. I could never understand why the other mechanics made judgments about me just because of my gender. I admit not all women are capable of performing mechanical skills; neither are men; some are very capable; others lack the qualifications, knowledge, or talent for this line of work.

Given the time period (mid 1980s), connecting with male mechanics proved taxing for a female mechanic. Even though women had made considerable strides during the previous century, many men were still not willing to allow a female to work by their side, preferring to act like children throwing a tantrum. However, I made friends with two fellow mechanics (out of the ten who worked there) during my first few weeks, while the other male co-workers made it their mission to rid me from the building.

It was very clear from the beginning that I needed to be prepared for a tough battle of the sexes – that my mere presence was not going to be accepted with open arms.

Each day, my supervisor handed me my assignment, which often would require a repair initiated by a day shift mechanic. One day, I was assigned to finish the engine installation for one of the buses that Gary from dayshift was working on.

As I approached the bay he was working in, I said, "Gary, I have been given the task to continue where you are leaving off on this bus."

Gary angrily replied, "No woman is going to touch the work I have done. Go find something else to do."

I did not retreat at his attempt to intimidate me. Instead, I asserted, "If you have a problem with this, you need to go and speak with the supervisor."

Gary dropped his tools and marched over to Harry, who was sitting at his desk.

"Look, Harry, I am not about to allow a woman to put her hands on my work. This is my assignment, and I refuse to instruct her on what is left to finish."

Harry stood his ground. "I have given Teresa this assignment because I need that bus done by end of shift this evening. The other mechanics are busy doing their assignments, and this one is hers. End of story."

Gary stood there for a moment in sheer disbelief that he had to bow down to allowing a woman to touch his masterpiece.

"Fine!" Gary spat out.

After I had waited in the work bay for Gary to return from his confrontation with Harry, Gary – his voice dripping with disgust – gave me the short version of the final repairs and packed up his tools. Then he punched out, usually the last step an employee takes before leaving the premises. But not this time.

Heading over to retrieve my toolbox, I noticed Gary doing something under the bus in question. (It was hard to see exactly what he was up to from my vantage point.) Gary then punched out and left the premises.

On the basis of his behavior and his hostility towards women, I suspected that there might be some sabotage in the works. I felt that his behavior was grounds for a good "once over."

As I glanced at the engine's top, sides and underside, I grabbed the oil filter to insure it was completely seated and tightened correctly. There it was: the one thing Gary was sure I would not check: the oil filter had been loosened enough to allow oil to spill out during the engine start-up, causing it to seize. Before I gave the filter a good turn to tighten it, I summoned my supervisor over to verify what I had observed.

By the end of shift, I had finished reassembling the engine, had started it up for the initial break–in period, and had reinstalled the hood on the bus. At that point, I took the bus out for a test drive. It purred like a kitten.

The next morning, Gary arrived, expecting to find the engine seized and his claims against my qualifications amply solidified. He asked one of the other dayshift mechanics where the bus in question might be found. He even mentioned that the engine should have seized. But instead of me, he was in fact the one in trouble. The Director of Transportation was aware of what occurred and was ready to address this offense with Gary.

Gary was furious to find that his dirty work had backfired. Although one would think some sort of punishment would follow, Gary just received a verbal warning that such conducted had better never happen again.

Now all the other mechanics who opposed me knew I was onto them, so they considered it imperative to change their approach in attempting to discredit me.

From this point on, every day brought a new issue concocted by this gang of males in order to make trouble for me – their hostility having been aggravated by frequent requests by school bus drivers that I be assigned to work on their buses. In spite of the supportive intentions of the drivers, their preference for my work only made more trouble for me.

At first this expression of loyalty seemed flattering, and I was happy to oblige. But as time went on, the male mechanics took these requests to suggest that they were less capable of their duties than I was -- which only intensified the situation.

Adding fuel to this conflict was the interest that local and out of state newspapers were showing in interviewing me about my experience as the first female heavy duty mechanic in the state. However, I was reluctant to accept the offers, because I did not want to create the appearance that I was better than the others; I just wanted to do my job the best I could.

Since the school district was not always receiving favorable media attention, I was approached by upper staff to consider the interview offers and to portray the district as a fair place to work. But I was still afraid that if I went ahead with the interviews, the tension would only increase, with me taking the brunt of it. The district assured me that they would not allow that to happen and that they would explain why they were encouraging all the media attention. Famous last words!

After thinking about it for a day, I decided to accept the offers and allow the interviews to occur. My main reason for doing so was to allow other women or girls who might be considering this career an opportunity to hear from one who has traveled that road.

The ensuing interviews soon seemed endless; I was interviewed by local and out-of-state newspapers, was offered an adult teaching seminar on automotive basics, and appeared on all local TV stations. In the end, I had been correct: the situation only became worse.

This celebrity-hood only added to all the harassment, disrespect, and torment I was receiving from some. In the beginning of my mechanical career, I never expected this type of behavior; I knew the road ahead would not come without a price, but I never imagined the magnitude of that price.

There were many days when I felt like giving up and flying the white flag of surrender; but, when I woke up the next morning, defeat was not an option. It was hard for me to comprehend all the hatred and hostility that some of my male co-workers harbored towards women in their work space. I kept trying to examine my own behavior in order to ascertain how I might have elicited this sort of outcome. But I just couldn't. Each day brought a new booby trap, and being on my toes was at the top of my daily agenda. It was exhausting to have to use so much of my energy playing defense.

This work environment proved very challenging and stressful – always trying to do my best, only for my efforts to be received as never good enough. For example, if I were to ask co-workers for assistance in lifting a large item, then I was criticized as weak; yet they would not hesitate to do the same when in need of help, in which case the subject of strength never came up.

On several occasions, I arrived for work to find my toolbox barricaded with boxes, blocking access to the box until I removed them. On other occasions my boots were stolen out of my locker and thrown in the trash.

This conflict focused not on a person working as a mechanic but on a woman insolently infiltrating the Boys' Club – a place the members held sacred and untouchable by a female. Within the Boys' Club it is not permissible to admit that a woman is capable of performing the duties of a mechanic or, for that matter, of any position that the "boys" felt was exclusively their domain.

Although not all of the male employees agreed with the majority, dissenters, unfortunately, felt the apparent need to remain silent. Had they stepped up and done what was right, then war would have been declared on them as traitors, numbering their days with the district.

At that time, I was keeping a daily journal – not to document what was occurring at work but just as a future reference. Little did I know that these journals would serve me well a little later on.

Because of the turmoil stirring in the shop, the Director of Transportation took it upon himself to find out just who I was and what my personal mission might be. Accordingly, he occasionally hired me to make needed repairs to his personal vehicles after hours. At first I wondered why he was going out of his way to choose me, when, previously, one of the male mechanics had been his choice to do these repairs.

In any case, I accepted the offers and took care of the needed repairs. The Director even made it a point to stand by and chat with me as I did the work.

When the mechanic I had replaced got wind of the fact that I was now repairing the Director's vehicles, he became very upset and addressed the issue with the Director. Nevertheless, I continued to be chosen when a repair was required. On one of these occasions, while the Director was observing my performance, he explained why he decided to inquire as to my ability and to find out what I was really made of.

It was gratifying to hear that, after our numerous interactions he realized that I was not at all what some of the males had portrayed me to be – in fact, quite the opposite. It was at that moment, that he acknowledged that the staff was in for a long battle of the sexes.

In spite of this gloomy prediction, the District did have anti-harassment policies and procedures but was failing to enforce them. As the first female to have ever entered into a predominately male position within the District, I was presenting the District with quite a challenge in managing a situation that was new territory for them.

After I had spent a couple of years trying to survive relentless harassment, the District transferred me to the North yard, from the Central yard where I had been working – where the hostility had been increasingly more intense. I was moved to the new yard in hopes of removing me from the hostile work environment, while an investigation was being conducted into my allegations towards some co-workers. This investigation was brought to Human Resources attention by the Director of Transportation. He knew this situation could not be handled at the shop level, so he approached HR to investigate.

The only problem with transferring me to the North yard was that some of the very same co-workers that had waged war on my existence in the shop also had been transferred. I was asked by the Director to do my best with the situation and to await the outcome of the investigation.

I arrived each day to work in hopes for a better day, trying to do my best and giving my all to work well with everyone. However, my direct supervisor, a particularly skilled mechanic, was not a fan of women in the shop. I found him inclined to say supportive things to my face, only to hear later about his verbal attacks on me behind my back.

My life was going in many directions; it was hard to keep up. Day after day of being mentally beaten takes a toll on one's soul. I begin to doubt myself and my destiny; but, as hard as it all was, I never lost sight of where I wanted to go in life.

While the investigation into my allegations against my co-workers was in the hands of Human Resources, I was anxious to learn their findings. I began to second-guess myself as I tried to work through the problems in one-on-one meetings with my co-workers in the presence of our supervisor. My efforts were unsuccessful, because the others were fixated on my occasional requests for help – as opposed to any complaints about my ability.

Finally the day scheduled for the report arrived, and I was summoned to my supervisor's office. There I was met by two representatives from Human Resources and my supervisor.

Emotions consumed me as the Human Resource personnel began to read their findings:

According to our findings into the allegations of a hostile work environment, we, Human Resources, have discovered that in fact you have been treated unfairly, in a hostile manner by fellow co-workers, with a few of the co-workers admitting to observing this misconduct.

It is our findings that although these allegations are true, we are not able to correct the issues at hand.

My blood began to boil; I held back the tears, and despair filled my insides.

I asked myself, *How this could be? They indicate that all is true, but nothing can be done? So all those workplace policies mean nothing and these men can continue to behave as they see fit?*

I said to everyone in the office, "Thanks for nothing." Grabbing the report, I ran into the women's bathroom.

Once inside, my emotions exploded. I began to sob – which is not like me, but I was at the end of my rope. This is the exact type of response the men were expecting from a woman. I knew I had to release in private. Grief-stricken and wounded, I had to pull myself together. It was at that moment that a bus driver entered the restroom and came to my rescue with generous expressions of support. After I had allowed her to read the report findings, she said she could not believe what had just happened.

I knew I could not finish out the day; I felt as if all the wind had been sucked out of me and my insides ripped apart. But if I ran, I would appear weak and not strong enough to handle the results of my journey so far. So, I finished out the day as best I could. Not wanting to talk to a soul – without even enough energy left in me to crack a smile – I found that day's night to be endless.

It was a good thing I had never acquired a taste for alcohol; otherwise, I would have been found on the floor, smashed. Instead, I sat in the dark, listening to music, brooding.

I returned to work the next day and tried my best to act as if nothing had happened, even though I wanted to take each one of those guys out back and beat the snot out of them. But what would that have gotten me besides trouble and descent to their level? My only options were either to run from it all or else not allow the others to dictate whether I was going to continue to work there. If I were to leave, they would have won. But I was not a quitter.

There are times when a small glimmer of hope and acceptance shines brightly, breaking the spill of being an evil outcast. One afternoon as I was arriving for my shift, I noticed Orville Smart, a field supervisor, chatting with the Director of Maintenance about servicing his company vehicle. Orville (or the Big O as I called him) was insistent that only a man could perform the needed service. The director, Marty, shook his head while Orville handed him the keys and informed Marty that he would return in a week. After the Big O departed the building, Marty called me over and instructed me to perform the service and check another problem Orville's car was experiencing.

I protested, "But, Sir, Orville was very specific about not allowing me to work on his car. Are you sure you want me to do it?"

"Yes. Go to work," Marty replied.

I knew that if Orville were to find out that I had worked on his car, all hell would break lose, so I maintained my silence in hopes of staying under Orville's radar. After I had completed the needed repairs, the car ran like new.

It was a week later on a Monday afternoon when Orville arrived to retrieve his car. Marty gladly gave him the keys, and Orville went out to check it over. Knowing that I was going to take the heat for working on his car if he found out, I kept out of sight.

All of a sudden, Orville reappeared, clearly on the hunt for Marty. My blood pressure began to elevate; someone might have tipped Orville off about my handling the repairs. Once he found Marty, I couldn't hear the conversation, but it looked a bit intense. At that moment, Orville turned and looked right at me. I knew I was in for it.

Orville started in my direction, but the look on his face did not appear to be one of disgust. Apparently trying to figure out what to say or explain, Orville offered his hand to me with an apparently sincere apology for doubting my ability as a mechanic.

"Teresa, I am so sorry for ever doubting you because you're a woman. I have been proven wrong. My car has never run so well, and I owe it all to you. I only want you to work on my car from here on out."

Wow. Considering the source, I took that message as a huge compliment. I guess there was hope for me yet. (Experiences like this invariably renew my self-confidence.) After that moment, I felt the highest respect for Orville, not because of his previous skepticism towards female mechanics but because he saw the worth in someone who had proved herself. For the moment, I saw this as a huge step toward gender equality.

The moment was short-lived, however, having apparently led a few holdout mechanics to feel abandoned by Orville and offended by this blow to their male egos. No matter how well I performed, I would never be good enough to change the minds of these co-workers.

Still, not all men I worked with were out to destroy my dream. One co-worker, Denny –soft spoken, reliably kind, and always helpful – never failed to speak to me during the change from his shift to mine. I thought that maybe here is a man who has a mind of his own and wants to form his own opinion of me in my own right. What better way to do so than to engage in conversation?

Before too long, Denny introduced me to his son one weekend and even asked me to accompany him to an event or two as friends. But with all that was happening, I wasn't about to let my guard down. Never knowing who was my friend or foe, I was always on my toes.

Months went on, and our friendship was becoming the center of conversation at work. The comments were getting personal and suggestive. Although my co-workers comprised a wide range in ages, I could see no such range in their maturity level: they were all equally threatened by the change reflected in the acceptance of a female into their version of the Boys' Club.

I could tell that the issue was bothering Denny, but I held out hopes that he was strong enough to endure the pressure. But the nasty comments were becoming more intense.

"You must be sleeping with her, which is why you are paying her attention. So tell us what she is like. You must be using her, and then once you are finished with her, you will drop her like a hot potato."

These innuendoes infuriated me. I was not a promiscuous person. I held strong values and morals; I have never been an easy mark. If these Neanderthals thought I was there looking for a hookup, they had guessed wrong. In fact, I was independent and always made it a point to never date someone I worked with, especially not when I was the center of attention. Having my personal life out there for everyone to judge and pick at has never been my idea of a happy life.

Denny began to show signs of distancing himself from me. His daily *hellos* and chit-chat were diminishing. By this time, my gut sensed that the harassment he was receiving for becoming friends with the "enemy" was affecting him.

My hunch was correct; this wouldn't be a friendship that Denny could maintain. These men were adult bullies waging war on their own kind for not sharing their beliefs.

Society focuses so intently on younger bullies; what about the adults who bully? Here is a prime example. It is OK to have our own opinions and beliefs, but to force them on others through bullying differs little from the conduct exhibited by misbehaving children.

I was disappointed to find that Denny could not stand up for what he believed in, instead bowing to peer pressure – a major component of bullying, a serious problem in our country, no matter the age group.

Disappointed or otherwise, I wasn't about to let Denny off scot free; I approached him one afternoon while preparing for my workday and asked, "So Denny, what's the deal? You rarely speak to me anymore. Have these other so-called men been getting to you?"

Hesitating, Denny replied, "Well, Teresa, I can't be your friend anymore; the other guys are getting on me for being friends with you, and I have to say goodbye."

"Denny, you will allow others to tell you who you can be friends with and who is acceptable to them?

You're right, we need to say goodbye, I want true friends, not temporary ones who can't handle the heat!"

We no longer spoke after that – not because I harbored any hostility toward Denny, but because if anyone exhibited friendship toward me, he would become the target of ridicule. A sad and frustrating fact about the fear of change (in this case, the acceptance of women in male-dominated work places) is that it affects not only women but men as well. Denny is a perfect example. In the end he couldn't be true to himself, because he himself ended up bullied and abused for temporarily accepting me.

It takes strong, determined souls with considerable integrity to buck prevailing norms. In all fairness, Denny did try; but, in the end, the adverse pressure proved to be too much for him. His weakness begs the question: how many of us are afraid to stand up for what we think is right in fear of becoming outcasts ourselves?

What opportunities, friendships, or collaborations have been destroyed because of this unreasonably fearful way of thinking? Unrestrained fear negatively impacts not only the lives of women but those of men as well – and, until fear is replaced with courage, nothing will change.

Denny's betrayal created more tension within me. I knew that my circle of friends at work was getting smaller. In response, I built an emotional barrier, tough and strong, around myself, not allowing others to get too close lest I be hurt again.

My distance to the other co-workers surely appeared to be snobbish or standoffish, when in fact, it was my protection. This was a hard way to work and live at a place you spent over eight hours a day. There were many times when I wondered if I had made the right decision to be a mechanic. As the pressure on me intensified, I never understood the magnitude of it all . . . until a few years later when my world came tumbling down.

Even the strong can fall.

IT TAKES A TOLL

After experiencing years of hostility and ostracism at the bus yard, I could tell that the accompanying stress– in addition to the aftermath of being shot – were beginning to take a toll on my health. I wasn't sleeping well, I wasn't eating as I should, and my attitude towards men was beginning to sour to a level to which it had never before sunk.

I am sure that if you had asked my male co-workers at the time – the ones who wore the war paint, puffed up their chests, and stomped around aggressively marking their territory – they would have expressed a very different basis for their hostility than mere male chauvinism. Clearly, the shooting had brought me even more attention than that which had already alienated them, creating even more distance between us. Every inquisitive visit from District employees, every interview request, every news story, set me up in the eyes of my co-workers as a *prima ballerina* who had been raised to a lofty status far above them.

My truth and my mission was not intended to attack these men; rather, it was a continuing effort to get them to accept a woman who wanted to pursue a career in automotive repair. But no matter how hard I tried, no matter what I did, no matter how good my work was, I couldn't break through.

Overall, it took fifteen-plus years of being told I didn't belong; told I couldn't do the job; told I was worthless; told that I only belonged in the kitchen, pregnant – my work over-scrutinized and double, triple checked – that I finally made my first big mistake. And then all hell broke loose.

While fueling the buses one day, I mistakenly put diesel fuel in a gasoline powered bus. This caused the bus to break down and require a tow back to the shop. Very shortly, I was called into the boss's office.

"Teresa I need to talk to you about the bus that just broke down. You were the last one to fuel it," he said.

"Okay. What happened?"

"Well, it seems that diesel was put into the gas tank when you were fueling it this morning. You know that particular bus requires gasoline. They had to remove some of the fuel and it was definitely diesel, not gasoline. Care to explain what happened?"

Standing there for a moment, going through my every move that morning, I couldn't even think straight. My mind was numb, and I grew angry inside.

This was the moment when the straw broke the camel's back for me. I could no longer keep it together: the stress, the pressure of trying to fit in, the abusive remarks and treatment – and now this. I hit rock bottom. I blew up.

"I can't do this anymore, everything about this place is so wrong. Because I'm a woman, I am being shut out. I am not allowed to fit in. I have tried my hardest to please everyone here, but it is never enough for all you bastards. I have had it!" I yelled at the top of my lungs.

"Calm down, Teresa. Calm down," he responded in a patronizing manner.

"Calm down? You're asking me to calm down when all I want to do is go punch every one of those so called men in the face!" I continued, "I am at the end of my rope. Calm down? Sure I'll calm down; you bet I'll calm down!"

At that point I stormed out of the office.

Heading straight to the woman's bathroom, again, I began to cry, amidst a few female bus drivers. Fortunately, the bus drivers in the bathroom at the time were supportive and kind.

After gaining my composure and exiting the bathroom, I was ordered by my supervisor to punch out for the day and await for a call from headquarters.

Receiving the expected call not long after arriving home, still very upset, I was informed that an appointment had been scheduled for me to visit the school psychologist. One mistake, one moment of telling my truth, and I was the one in need of psychiatric help!

Obviously at the end of my rope and upset, I was quickly pigeonholed by human resources as "disturbed." I was disturbed, all right – disturbed with the way non-traditional women were treated in the workplace. Now – adding insult to injury – they wanted to make me out as crazy.

The next week I found myself in the psychologist's office, where I was greeted by the secretary, who just happened to be my girlfriend and

213

neighbor, Betty. (On a few occasions, I had confided in her about my ongoing work situation.) Betty started telling me that Human Resources had called their office about a crazy employee whom they wanted Dr. Arnold, Betty's boss, to see. It suddenly dawned on her that the person human resources were referring to was me. We nervously laughed at her surprise but understood the seriousness.

The subsequent sessions were focused on my work situation, as well as my understanding of what was happening in the shop and the reasons why. It took only three appointments for Dr. Arnold to conclude that I was, in fact, the victim of a hostile work environment.

The Doctor informed me that I should file a lawsuit in order to force the District to follow their own policies and procedures. At first, I felt this might be a setup. With all my past experiences, what else was I to think? With my clouded mind, it was hard to determine who I could trust. I felt reassured, however, when Betty asserted that Dr. Arnold was a fair and honest man.

Here is where my daily journals would become an important element of my case.

After filing suit, I found myself on administrative leave – without pay, essentially unemployed.

The suit took two years before a federal judge ruled that there enough evidence to prove a hostile work environment did exist and the District would pay me an undisclosed amount for my suffering.

This apparent victory still did not change anything at the school district. It only meant that the taxpayers

214

had paid me off and that I was once again out of a job – but not out of a career. For me, it was not about the money, ever! It was about what is right and about the prerogative of anyone to be allowed to perform a job regardless of gender.

I even told the judge, "If the school district would actually enforce some of their own harassment policies, preventing another situation like this from arising in the future, I would be happy to take only a dime as payment."

In response, the judge was quick to tell me that that isn't how it works in America. We fix things with monetary judgments, which I received. It is still so hard for me to believe that employers and corporations have policy and procedures in place which many still choose to ignore. In many ways I was lucky, because it was ultimately the school district that had brought the hammer down on themselves by sending me to their psychologist in response to my legitimate workplace complaints.

Yes, I chose this profession, and with it came resistance. But if policies are in place for the protection of employees, then why was it unacceptable to enforce them? No wonder so many people are hesitant to step forward when they are being mistreated or harassed.

After two years of going through the court process and coming out of it on top, it took me another two years to finally seek employment in the field I love, mechanics. As a result, I found a wonderful company that hired me as fleet manager overseeing a department operating over 300 units.

It did not take me long to settle into my new job and begin to feel as one of the family. But acceptance did not come without initial reservations on the part of the company's owner – further evidence that no matter where I was employed, I would be under the microscope before being accepted for my knowledge.

A huge advantage for me with this company was my lengthy connection with the Sheriff's Office. As a commissioned Deputy, I brought more to the table than mere mechanical skills; I also offered my knowledge and experience in law enforcement. It took me awhile, but I finally won the acceptance of the company's owner and managed to become good friends with the Chief Financial Officer.

In addition, I was able to hire a team of qualified men free of Texas-sized egos. (In spite of all my hopes, I never had a woman apply.) While I still found myself struggling for acceptance by some of the male managers, once it was known that the company's owner had my back, my position grew to a level of high importance.

A NEAR MISS

In spite of the favorable results of my issues with the school district, my life was a tornado swirling around me with no escape. I longed to find a sense of normality, since my life represented anything *but*. Yes, I had chosen my life, but I never really knew the obstacles I would encounter along the way or how draining they would be.

I was on a roller coaster between my energizing progress with the Sheriff's Office and the demoralizing conflicts with my co-workers at the school district – the latter wearing me down exhausting me. The only reprieve I could find was in my personal life. I enjoyed my time alone; I could breathe. The solitude helped me to regain my peace and drive.

Early in my life I had always felt that marriage was not for me, an aversion attributable not so much to the types of men who surrounded me but to my own preference. Although I wasn't sure why I felt that way, I had been expressing that attitude since I was little. I still dated of course, with a few men wanting more out of the relationship; but the mix just was never right, and settling down was never in my cards.

Many of the men I dated were intimidated by my ambitions toward male-dominated professions as well as by my independence. I could care for myself; I never needed anyone to take care of me – a level of self-reliance that most men simply could not accept. On a few occasions the issue resulted in questions like "What can I give you that you cannot give yourself?" My response was always, "Well, how about *you*?"

For awhile I dated a gentleman, Tom Simpson, who had been a great supporter of my mission. A journalist by profession, he suggested that I produce a video for women in order to teach them basic auto repair. He kept on me for months to pursue this innovative idea.

In following up on the video plan, I discovered that one of the Sheriff's sergeants was married to the owner of a video production business. To my surprise, the pieces were naturally falling into place; things felt right. At this point I had been writing an automotive column for a Florida newspaper, *The Happy Herald*, for the past year – their first female automotive columnist. An automotive video would enhance my female-education mission and wouldn't look bad on a resume either.

Further pursuing this plan, I found a few sponsors to help with the cost of the video's production, which proceeded smoothly. The video was a sales success at local shops throughout Nevada, helping shine healing rays of hope into my life at a time when I needed them most. And I was blessed with a further bonus in the sense that Tom had persuaded me to teach auto mechanics for the Parks and Recreation Department, which I did for a few years.

A worthy man, Tom never needed to compete with me; we were equals. His confidence was refreshing, and I was grateful for the time we spent together. Eventually, however, Tom grew itchy for bigger things in his life, and he ended our relationship in order to follow his dreams. I was sad to see him depart, but I would be the last one to try to stop someone from finding his rainbow. Too many had tried to do the same thing to me!

During the period when I was dating Tom, I became friends with one of the maintenance supervisors at the school district, Johnny Jones. We had a common interest in classic cars, which we discussed in considerable detail whenever he wandered into the maintenance shop.

One day, Johnny asked me to join a car club of which he was a member. Working swing shift, I found it hard to attend their meetings, held every third Wednesday at 6 p.m. However, I was able to attend one of the meetings after I asked my supervisor if I could take a later lunch than usual.

The meetings were held at a local pizza parlor not far from the bus shop. As soon as I entered the meeting room, Johnny quickly greeted me, after which I ended up sitting between Johnny and a male about my age. I said my *hello*s, and that was that, because I was able to stay for only a portion of the meeting before having to head back to work.

A few weeks later, I received a call from the male stranger who had sat quietly next to me at the club meeting.

"Hi. Is this Teresa?"

"Yes. Who's this?"

"I am not sure if you remember me, but we met at the club meeting a few weeks back. This is Wayne Carson," he answered.

"Were you the quiet one sitting next to me?"
He chuckled, "Yes, that was me."

Have you ever heard a voice that seemed to enable you to correctly size up the caller? Here was a sincere voice inquiring about a mirror for a classic vehicle. The voice's owner indicated that he had been told by my friend Johnny that I had a great line on classic car parts.

We chatted for over an hour about everything except a mirror until the very end. Unaware that I was not in the mood for dating, Wayne broached the subject by lamenting about his dissatisfying dating experiences. I responded sympathetically to him, indicating that the men I had met had been generally not worth keeping – not because they were bad people but because we weren't a good fit.

I almost passed up the chance to go out with Wayne. But my cousin, Linda, persuaded me to at least go on a first date with him. I thought about that idea for a few days, realizing Linda was right; so the next time Wayne called, ostensibly about his mirror but really to ask me out, I accepted.

Continuing the mirror ruse, I recommended a source for a mirror that turned out to be of such good quality that, after 33 years, Wayne not only still has that mirror but me too – the latter acquisition having taken us 20 years to accomplish.

For us, there was no urgency to marry; things were perfect just the way they were. Waiting for the right guy was well worth the wait, especially since I hadn't even been looking. Wayne had arrived as a bright star in the darkness of my life at the time – a true blessing in every sense of the word. He has never felt the need to compete with me; he is comfortable in his manly skin, accepting me for me – a capability possessed by very few of the men I have known.

Meeting Wayne was like a gift from God, especially considering that when we first met, he had two young boys that he loved deeply. Dating Wayne also meant his boys were a huge part of the package.

Our relationship started off slowly, and we faced many challenges along the way. But as we grew to love each other, we found ways around obstacles threatening our happiness.

Wayne and I had much in common, especially when it came to our mechanical aptitude. He loved tinkering with cars as a hobby, while I love repairing them as a profession.

My husband notably reminds me of my dad, who was intently meticulous about everything, including house cleaning. Wayne is not afraid of what others think about his desire to keep a very orderly home; he does all the laundry and manages to keep every car he owns well- maintained and sparkly clean – just like my dad did.

This match has been the crown jewel of my life.

Heaven can wait.

WHEN TWO WORLDS COMBINE

In spite of Wayne's complete acceptance of me as an equal, my fight for equality in the workplace was still not over; there were a few male managers that were not at all happy that I was among them. One in particular, Mathew, made it clearly known that he would see to it that my days as Fleet Manager would be numbered. But, I took this hostility in stride, because the one thing I had learned from the few mechanic jobs that I held was how to handle those men who were still living in the dark ages, convinced that men were the superior gender.

With this new job, both of my careers would come in to play often, sometimes daily. My years on the Police force gave me a great sense of suspicious situations and how to deal with them. Having the keen eye for things that look out of place or wrong was a skill I conquered many years earlier.

With every new job, I held hopes of breaking the mold and being accepted as one of the team, not considered an outcast. One would think – considering the war that men have waged on me or other women in the workplace – that I, given the pain, loneliness, and intimidation, would have quit. I have to admit that I often considered throwing in the towel, although I knew that *giving in* meant *giving up.* That was not an option for me. This job was no exception; I learned early on, that my sense of suspicion was extremely reliable – especially concerning a male co-manager who made it clear that my mere presence was not acceptable to him.

Over time, I began to suspect that the manager, Mathew, was up to something but just could not put my finger on just exactly what that was. However, I knew that in time things would fall into place.

At first it was hard for me to pinpoint what exactly was amiss with him. But there were indicators that made the cop inside me take notice, such as the times no one could locate him on a jobsite or his refusal to answer his company phone.

I would show up on a job location only for him to seem impatient for me to depart. He even went so far as to insist that I notify him when I would have the need to visit.

My every move was scrutinized by Mathew. Although he was not any type of supervisor of mine, he still had an in with his boss. Once, I was asked by one of the construction crew if I wanted a perfectly good tree that had been removed and would live if I just took good care of it, placing it in some really good dirt for a few months. I arrived on the job site to pick up the tree, and, as I was leaving, Mathew observed me with a tree in the back of my company vehicle. Since he was always looking for an opportunity, he used this one to contact the company's main office and inform them that I had stolen a tree from one of the sites.

Soon I was summoned to the office to meet with the CFO, Dave, who was investigating why I had a tree in the back of my truck. I advised him of the foreman who contacted me about the tree. The CFO contacted the foreman who indeed confirmed that I was given the tree that would have gone into the garbage.

During weekly managers' meetings, the general manager was occasionally unable to attend. Whenever

223

that occurred, one of the upper managers would cover his spot overseeing the meeting. On one particular day, Mathew was assigned the lead for the meeting, to which I always arrived early in order to insure that I was able to obtain my favorite seat in the conference room.

After a few of the other managers arrived, Mathew entered the room. The look on his face was one of pure sarcastic delight. He turned to me, approached the chair I was seated in, placed his hands on the armrests of the chair, looked directly into my face, and got close enough for me to feel his disgusting breath.

At this point, Mathew declared, "Today is your day, Teresa." Then he turned, laughing, and walked away.

My head was spinning, trying to think of the dirty deed he was planning in his male chauvinistic mind. The meeting began, and, as I had figured, I was topic of discussion, led by none other than Mathew. Aware that he held the lead in the meeting and commanded power over my position as well, I was prepared to neutralize anything he could conjure up in trying to destroy my credibility.

He started right in with the claim that my automotive ability and knowledge were not up to par and that many of the landscape teams were afraid to operate the company trucks because they felt repairs done by my team placed their lives in danger. Mathew asked the other male managers to chime in to validate his claim. Since I was the only female manager on staff at the time, it was as if he felt empowered because of my gender.

Little did he know that not all the other managers were playing into his plan. Mathew became a bit angry when a few of the others actually stated they were pleased with the way the shop personnel cared for the equipment and with their attentiveness to time restraints on the jobs.

This did not stop Mathew; he had plan B in his back pocket. He spouted out that his team would no longer bring their vehicles to the shop or contact me when a breakdown occurred. He had instructed his team to take them to an outside vendor.

I had had enough female bashing for one day. I jumped from my chair, sending it flying behind me and hitting the wall; the look on my face was of anger and disgust. My right hand hit the table, bringing attention to everyone in the room. A deafening silence descended while all eyes turned towards me.

There was a crackle in my voice as my octaves elevated. I looked directly at Mathew, and then, I let loose.

"How dare you accuse me of endangering others, obviously in hopes of getting them on your side and getting me fired? What are you so afraid of, Mathew, your inability to do your job? Or maybe you have something to hide and riding me from here will allow you to continue with whatever dirty work you are involved in? Or maybe you are the one who is insecure and in fear of a woman doing a better job than you are able to do? I bet if I had a set of balls between my legs, we would not be having this conversation.

"Well, let me tell you all this: I am not leaving. I do know my job, and, if you are involved in any type of criminal activity, I will hunt you down. You can count on that. And you call yourselves men. Keep looking behind your backs, gentlemen, because I will be in your shadows."

I stormed out of the room and headed directly over to the CFO's office. He was alone working on some issues when I barged into his office and explained, in a decidedly irate tone, that I had had it with the other managers and that something had better be done about it. As I turned to exit, I informed him that I was so angry that I was going home to cool off. Moving quickly down the office stairs, I encountered my boss, Jay, who asked how things were going. That was a big mistake; I let him have it on what had transpired during the managers meeting and told him that I was leaving for the day.

The next day, I returned somewhat calmer than I had been the previous afternoon. Immediately, my boss and Dave summoned me to the latter's office. What I was about to hear was not only disappointing but infuriating as well. Jay sympathized with Mathew, asserting that I was in fact out of control and needed some counseling. Further, Jay had set up a meeting for me with an anger management company to help me handle my aggressions. Although I was totally blown away to learn that Jay and Dave felt that I was out of control, I thought *Fine. If that is what they want, so be it.*

My first meeting with Dee Shaw, a psychologist specializing in anger management, took place at her home in order to analyze why my temper had flared. Dee was a very patient individual, and, after hearing the facts, she exhibited an excellent understanding of the situation. Without coming right out and saying so, she made it clear that she was not a fan of Mathew's either.

Dee had been hired a few months early by the company to hold a teamwork seminar for all managers, so I had a bit if foreknowledge about who she was. Further, Dee had also had the opportunity at that time to interact with all managers, including Mathew.

Our meetings went on for over four weeks, resulting in a report indicating that the presence of a female in a nearly all-male company had led to feelings of betrayal on the part of some of the males in reaction to the company's placement of her in a high position, that is, Maintenance Manager.

In any case, hostility from Mathew continued, and many other events took place through which Mathew tried to obtain enough evidence against me to lead the company to fire me. It took a meeting with the owner to persuade him that I was being set up. As a result, he immediately notified management that not only would I not be fired for the false allegations Mathew kept asserting, but that he, the owner, would be the only one authorized to even entertain the thought of doing so.

From that moment on, Mathew knew he was waging a war he could not win. Not long after this all took place, I received a call from the Sheriff's Office requesting my assistance in their search for an individual they were looking for – none other than Mathew, who was wanted for sexual assault. As indicated earlier, I had been sure that there was something suspicious about Mathew, and now precisely what that was had come to light. He had pursued my dismissal due to his fear that my affiliation with law enforcement would lead me to catch on to what he was involved in.

Following the arrest of Mathew, things seemed to settle down, and my job became a bit easier to perform without constantly having to look over my shoulder to see if Mathew was checking up on me.

Having been employed with the Nursery for almost ten years, I decided it was time to find new adventures. After leaving my Fleet Manager position at the Nursery, I took a job for one year at a trucking company. But it just was not the right fit for me. The company clearly wanted someone who could almost set up residence in the office.

Unfortunately for the company, I, after devoting many years of my career to long workdays, was not ready for a slavish work schedule.

WHERE DO I GO FROM HERE

Having left my job – and now finding myself unemployed – I decided to start a new phase in my life. It was time to change my focus from empowering myself to helping to empower other women. Although I had been working hard to gain knowledge, inner strength, and acceptance, that effort succeeded mostly in bringing me into close contact with the Boys' Club, a club that I had learned was not ready for female members.

Previously, I had held educational seminars and produced an automotive training video for women before video training had caught on. Further, during the previous thirty years, I had been writing a column for the Happy Herald, a newspaper intended to educate other women about their automobiles. However, I understood finding new terrain was a "must" in order to maintain my mark in today's social media frenzy. Even though I was computer savvy, I was not a fan of Facebook. Being hooked to a device daily – like needing a daily fix – was not my idea of a fun-filled day. (The internet was evolving faster and faster by the day, and keeping up with it has always been a full time job.)

It was during Thanksgiving of that year that my niece, Sonia Perozzi, daughter of my sister Ana, encouraged me to develop a website for Teresa's Garage (the d.b.a. I used for occasional contract work.) She made a good argument as to why I should bite the bullet and make the effort to establish my own website.

After I had proceeded as advised by Sonia, doors began to open. I found Facebook to be an ideal avenue for finding women sharing my passion for automobiles, racing, and other things in life. I began researching sites and women whose own accomplishments would be a great "read" for my followers. The start was slow, and I knew the one skill I needed in order to advance my knowledge was that of managing and maintaining my website. After I had ultimately gained that skill, I felt good about being able to release my niece from the website duties and carry the load myself, freeing Sonia up to handle her own affairs.

At this point I wanted time to regroup and ask myself, *Where do I go from here?*

After several months, I hit upon an idea to host a car show for female car owners – a day just for the ladies. I reached out to a local business in hopes of landing their location for the show. After a few conversations, the owner of a local restaurant offered me the use of her property. It was now time to start the planning.

Never having hosted a car show before, I was in search of what I would need in order to make it a success. As a participant in previous car shows, I had an inkling as to what they were about, but I wanted mine to be different from all the rest. No one was hosting a show just for the ladies; this would be a first for the area, and I wanted it to be unique.

At this point, a girlfriend jumped in to help, as did other friends once they learned that the show was on the calendar – with a new approach: women only. I used my website to attract followers to the show; but the best source of advertising was word of mouth. In addition, I contacted local businesses for raffle prizes in hopes of bringing in some cash for a local charity dedicated to women.

The day came for the show, and – although the numbers were small for the first time – the footprint had been established. We had received only twelve entrants, but everyone in attendance left with a big grin her face. This modest success gave me encouragement to push forward and make this car show a yearly event.

Later on, the show (now known as *Women with Wheelz*) found a home for three successive years at the National Automobile Museum in Reno, Nevada. Each year brought more entrants, and the ladies in attendance gained a sense of acceptance into the car-show scene, which men have dominated for years. This show represented a day just for them, and it did not matter what type of car they brought, whether new, old, or unfinished. It was a time for women to come together, and that they did.

In spite of the success of the *Women with Wheelz* car show, a larger task remained: that of incorporating a women-only event into Reno's major, internationally renowned, week-long annual car festival, Hot August Nights.

For several years, I had been attempting, without significant success, to interest Hot August Nights (aka HAN) in just such a women's event. However, matters began to change rapidly one day when a number of listeners of my radio show, *Teresa's Garage*, stormed HAN via email demanding a women-only event. The very next day, HAN invited me to present a proposal for a one-day women-only event to take place during the 2018 Show and Shine. Given only four days to prepare, I immediately began working the phones to form a team to develop a logo, logistics, and seminar preparations.

After having in fact accomplished that four-day miracle, I encountered a further challenge beyond merely putting on a car event: how to accommodate a previous request from Recycled Rides (a non-profit whose mission is to provide automobiles to needy recipients) that I partner with them by incorporating into the planned event a donation of a car to a deserving breast cancer patient.

Fortunately, the HAN people reacted positively to the proposal which I had presented, ultimately resulting in quite a successful event – so successful, in fact, that plans are currently afoot for a larger 2019 version, to include the donation of three cars to deserving recipients.

Shortly after that 2018 women-only car show, Virginia City (the famous historic nineteenth-century mining town near Reno) asked me to partner with them and bring my original *Women with Wheelz* car show to their town. (The show had outgrown the National Automobile Museum that had served us well for three years, and I knew it was time to find a larger location.) I gladly accepted their offer, and, once the change had been announced, the response – male and female – was overwhelming.

In addition to the pleasant surprise of Virginia City's invitation, 2018 proved to be a year of further recognition for my efforts. In March of that year, I was honored as Reserve Deputy of the Year for the entire country by the National Sheriff's Association. This prestigious award acknowledged my years of service as a Deputy – as well as my dedication in protecting and serving the people of Washoe County.

Further, 2018 brought notification that I would receive an award for my dedication to Outreach (a program through which the Sheriff's Office partners with local schools in order to enhance community understanding of the Department's roles). Having arrived at the ceremony, waiting for it to begin, I reflected back to my beginnings.

It felt good to have paid forward what had been given to me.

It's a Wrap

Rekindling my memories helps to serve as a remembrance for me about where I came from and how I arrived at who I am today. I was never the beautiful one (which was never a worry); I was the short one, the thin one, the quiet one; but I made up for those disadvantages in my adult years.

My childhood was far from lower-class, but I could never understand such classification of people anyway. Having money supposedly makes folks upper-class; but, from what I saw, wealth has completely the opposite effect – at least in terms of one's conduct. Exhibit A: Vivian Martin's family, who thought the air smelled better at their altitude than it did at mine.

Besides the attempted alienation wrought on me by the Martins, I soon faced a teacher trying to see that I knew my subordinate place as a female as well as the futility of my future plans, which she claimed were unreachable. This attempted discouragement made no more sense to me than the prejudice I had seen inflicted on my kindergarten teacher, Miss Moon.

Miss Moon was an outcast herself for having been born an African-American; yet, as a young child, all I knew was that she had a better tan than I did. I had no awareness of the issues concerning blacks and whites. But I learned later in life that I and Miss Moon had much in common: she, shunned because of her color, and I, shunned because of my gender. However, in spite of all that eluded my understanding, it was clear to me that Miss Moon was a respectful and inspiring teacher regardless of skin color.

I was further inspired by Mr. Hawkins, my art teacher, who believed in me while aiming at what all teachers should work toward: helping students pursue their passions and their talents.

And then there was Mike the mechanic, who helped convince me that my dreams were within reach by giving me opportunities to test the waters – as well as the confidence to win over a customer who had initially assumed that being female automatically disqualified me as a mechanic.

Along similar lines, I learned valuable lessons in connection with the drill team. Developing teamwork; polishing a finished product; meeting other girls with different dreams; we truly respected each other for who we were.

Likewise, the dog food plant was willing to take a chance on someone who represented change, knowing the turmoil it would create, yet giving me the opportunity to prove myself.

Meanwhile, the Sheriff's Office hired me to perform a dangerous job where many women feared to tread, while the Deputies helped mold a green 21-year-old female into the Deputy I am today. They were not afraid to teach a woman, nor where they in fear of a woman entering their domain. Seeing a person passionate about police work, they mentored me at every call and every arrest made – turning my mistakes into improvements. The support and encouragement these men offered continues even today, and I am blessed to know them. They truly have my back.

Although my time at the School district was depressing and hurtful, it was also a time of change – and with change comes pain, confusion, and fear. I represented all of that to my male co-workers, who were, for the most part, never able to handle the change nor willing to accept it – preferring instead to believe the toxic lie that a woman's place is barefoot, pregnant, and in the kitchen. I was a new breed of woman, and they were protesting.

That morning when I was shot in the line of duty could have ended horribly. Instead, the result was a young man opening his heart to send a kind message that helped me through a wrenching emotional experience – showing what a small act of kindness can do for another's heart.

Meeting my husband-to-be was a true blessing. Here was a man who never saw me as competition, nor was he offended because I was a cop/mechanic – nor insecure that I owned a house and could care for myself quite nicely. This man, secure in his own skin, is the right man for me. He is kind, hardworking, and willing to work as a team where others could not. He finds me interesting and unthreatening to his masculinity – a match made in heaven.

With all the attention I have received over the years, from being the first female in many male-dominated domains to the media-covered events in which I work as a Sheriff's Deputy, the effect on me could have been untoward. I might have developed into a self-centered snob condescending with the same snooty altitude as that of the Martins; instead, I try to use that recognition to make things better for all of those to whom I am responsible.

In spite of the adversities I have faced, I have tried to see that the lessons I have drawn from my experiences are positive and wise – always avoiding negativity, a cancer from which nothing good arises. I am no angel by any means, but I stand for law and order and for giving from my heart.

So, withal, I offer these thoughts: live your life your way, on your terms – not necessarily in the manner that society dictates. Connect with people who believe in you and who affirm your self-confidence. Find a dream, if you haven't done so already, and find a way to live that dream.

If you are going to leave footprints in life, leave prints worth following!

Teresa and David Cotter

Teresa receiving her Deputy of the Year Award

Teresa and Wayne early in their relationship

Teresa and Ron

About the Author

Teresa Aquila (*Author, Columnist, Mechanic, Radio Show Host, Deputy*)

Teresa Aquila is a renowned mechanic, radio show host, teacher, and producer of an auto repair video for women. Her career in mechanics has spanned over 43 years working as a self taught mechanic on everything from Porsches to heavy equipment in a domain dominated by men.

Teresa's love for automobiles came at a very early age, despite the discouragement of many including her mother. Self-driven, she rose to her dreams of one day being a police officer and automobile mechanic. Her mission shifted from empowering herself to empowering other women to pursue their dreams.

As a Reserve Deputy Sheriff for 42 years, Teresa has become a local icon. Ranging from being shot in the line of duty in 1988 to receiving a prestigious award as Reserve Deputy of the Year by the National Sheriff's Association in 2018, Teresa's experiences make for truly entertaining and inspiring reading.

About The Editor

Charlie Manes, bloodied but unbowed, is a retired high school English teacher who expended his prime promoting the power and beauty of the aptly-turned phrase – the perfect, exquisitely-chosen word – against onslaughts of teenage run-ons, comma-splices, *non-sequiturs,* and (horror of horrors), unending legions of the dreaded dangling participle.

Given that Charlie is not only a member in good standing with the Grammar Police but an avid classic car collector as well, he finds Teresa Aquila's tales of her dual path in law enforcement and automobilia not only supremely easy to relate with but enormously inspiring as well. He considers his part in polishing up her work to have been every bit equal in pleasure as burnishing the luster of an elegantly curvilinear fender whose sweeping lines beckon us back to the days when They Made Them Like They Used To.

Some things, he's sure you'll agree upon reading Teresa's memoir, They Still Do.

About the Co-Author

Sonia Perozzi, niece of Teresa Aquila, daughter of Linda Aquila, director of musical theater, writer of scripts, teacher of young and upcoming thespians, is elated to be making her debut as an editor with "Life Inside The Boys' Club."

When she was asked to be a part of this production, telling the story of her Aunt's life, she jumped at the opportunity, eager to learn more about the woman who influenced and inspired her growing up and continues to do so.

Sonia could regale you with all the memories and influences her Aunt Tee has had on her, but then she would be telling her story and she should write her own book. Instead, she will tell you the conviction, integrity, passion and drive her Aunt expresses in her life story is something she aspires to do within her own life.

Since working on this book Sonia has taken many a note from her Aunt applying them to lessons when teaching her students with wonderful results. Storytelling, in its many different forms, is Sonia's passion and she is grateful to have been a part of telling the story of such an amazing woman, who inspires, lifts and touches countless lives, including her own.

BRAVO!

_____

est capable de lire ce livre!

*À ma cousine Penny, qui n'a pas
une once de méchanceté en elle.
— J.O'C.*

*Aux vraies « chic filles » de ma vie –
elles se reconnaîtront.
— R.P.G.*

*À M. Girl, qui n'aurait pas
pu être plus gentille.
— T.E.*

Catalogage avant publication de Bibliothèque et Archives Canada

O'Connor, Jane
La fille agaçante / Jane O›Connor ;
illustrations, Robin Preiss Glasser ;
texte français d'Hélène Pilotto.

(Je lis avec Mademoiselle Nancy)
Traduction de: Fancy Nancy and the mean girl.
Pour les 5 à 8 ans.
ISBN 978-1-4431-2021-0

I. Preiss-Glasser, Robin II Pilotto, Hélène III. Titre. IV. Collection:
O'Connor, Jane. Je lis avec Mademoiselle Nancy

PZ23.O26Fil 2012   j813'.54   C2012-902441-4

Édition publiée par les Éditions Scholastic,
604, rue King Ouest, Toronto (Ontario) M5V 1E1,
avec la permission de HarperCollins.

5 4 3 2 1   Imprimé au Canada   119   12 13 14 15 16

MIXTE
Papier issu de
sources responsables
FSC® C103113
FSC
www.fsc.org

Je lis avec Mademoiselle

NANCY

La fille agaçante

Jane O'Connor

Illustration de la couverture : Robin Preiss Glasser
Illustrations des pages intérieures : Ted Enik
Texte français d'Hélène Pilotto

Éditions
SCHOLASTIC

Vendredi, il y aura des Olympiades à l'école. On fera des courses et un pique-nique. La plupart des élèves ont hâte, mais pas moi. Moi, je les redoute. (Redouter une chose, c'est en avoir peur.)

Mme Mirette distribue les tee-shirts.
Je ne suis pas dans la même équipe que
mes amis. Mais ce n'est pas pour cela
que je redoute les Olympiades.

Je préfère le tee-shirt rouge. (Préférer,
c'est aimer une chose plus qu'une autre.)
Mais ce n'est pas pour cela que je redoute
les Olympiades.

Je les redoute parce que je ne
cours pas vite. Je dois participer
à la course de relais. L'an
dernier, j'ai fait perdre
mon équipe. On a ri
de moi.

8

À la récréation, Gabrielle porte
son tee-shirt. Il est vert. Oh, non!
Nous sommes dans la même équipe!
Gabrielle est parfois malveillante.
(C'est un mot chic pour dire
« agaçante ».)

— Je fais la course de relais,

m'annonce Gabrielle. Et toi?

Je fais signe que oui.

Gabrielle dit :

— Zut! On va perdre, c'est sûr!

Chez moi, je regarde le bulletin météo. S'il pleut vendredi, les Olympiades seront annulées. Pas de chance : on annonce beau et chaud. Zut!

Peut-être qu'en m'exerçant, je serai
plus rapide. Je cours chaque jour
après l'école.

C'est inutile.

Je suis aussi lente qu'un escargot!

13

Jeudi, durant la récréation, j'entends
Gabrielle dire :

— Je suis avec Nancy dans la course
de relais. Mon petit frère court plus
vite qu'elle!

Ce n'est pas très gentil…

À midi, je n'ai pas d'appétit. (C'est
une façon chic de dire que je n'ai pas
faim.) Je ne finis même pas mon petit
gâteau. Les Olympiades ont lieu
demain. Je vais me couvrir de ridicule!
(Cela veut dire qu'on va rire de moi.)

Lionel est chanceux. Il s'est cassé
la jambe il y a deux semaines. Il ne
peut pas courir. Cela me donne une
idée formidable.

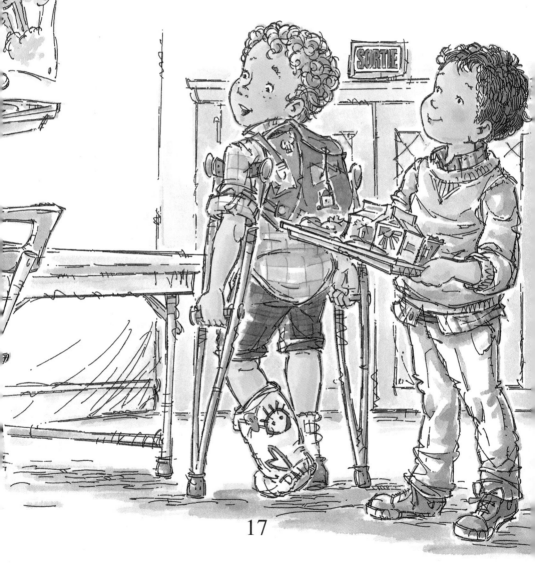

17

En rentrant à la maison, je fais semblant
de trébucher.

— Aïe! Aïe! Je me suis foulé la cheville!
(C'est un mot chic pour dire
qu'on s'est fait mal à la cheville.)

J'entre dans la salle à manger en boitant. Ma sœur m'aide à m'asseoir. Je dis à mes parents :

— Avec ma cheville, ce serait plus sage de ne pas courir demain. Vous devriez écrire un mot à Mme Mirette.

Plus tard, mon père vient me voir.

— Nancy, as-tu vraiment mal au pied?

— Pourquoi me demandes-tu ça? dis-je.

Mon propre père ne me croit pas!

— Eh bien, répond-il, parfois
tu boites d'un pied…
et parfois tu boites de l'autre.

Tout à coup, je me mets à sangloter.
(C'est comme pleurer, mais en plus
bruyant.) Je suis aussi mauvaise
menteuse que coureuse! Je raconte
tout à mon père : la course, Gabrielle.
Il comprend.
Nous parlons longtemps.

Le jour des Olympiades, je ne boite
pas. Je porte le tee-shirt de mon
équipe. J'ai même mis mes chaussettes
à froufrous pour me porter chance.
J'encourage mon équipe. (Je suis très
bonne pour encourager.)

23

C'est l'heure de la course de relais.
Je rejoins Gabrielle et lui parle
sans utiliser de mots chics.

— Je vais courir le plus vite possible, mais si on perd, je ne veux pas entendre de paroles blessantes. Tu es une bonne coureuse, mais une mauvaise perdante.

Gabrielle reste bouche bée! Ce qui veut dire qu'elle est tellement surprise qu'elle ne sait pas quoi dire.

La course de relais
commence. Gabrielle s'élance, court
jusqu'au cône et revient vers moi. Elle a
une bonne avance sur les autres coureurs.

27

Gabrielle arrive et me touche. À mon tour, je cours vers le cône. J'ai une bonne longueur d'avance.

Oh, non! Les autres coureurs me dépassent.

J'arrive dernière… comme l'an dernier.

Nous perdons la course.

Je me sens mal!

Pendant le pique-nique, Gabrielle vient
me voir. Oh, oooh! Que me veut-elle?
Elle me demande :

— Tu veux un biscuit? C'est ma mère
qui les a faits.

J'accepte et je la remercie.

Tout va bien.

J'ai même retrouvé l'appétit!

31

Les mots chics de Mademoiselle Nancy

Voici les mots chics du livre :

appétit : sensation de faim

malveillant(e) : qui veut du mal

préférer : aimer une chose plus qu'une autre

redouter : avoir peur de quelque chose

rester bouche bée : être surpris au point de
 ne plus parler

sangloter : pleurer bruyamment

se couvrir de ridicule : faire rire de soi

se fouler la cheville : se blesser à la cheville